D1076119

Citizens' Minds

The French Revolution

Jamie Byrom
Christine Counsell
Michael Riley

PEARSON

Longman

Citizens' Minds – The French Revolution

Introduction   4

'The blood you are to shed…'

Your enquiries

1 High hopes and big complaints

What was everyone complaining about in 1789?   6

2 'We will only leave at the point of Bayonets.'

What's the story behind the Tennis Court Oath?   26

3 Canon, muskets, fire and smoke

Why have such different stories been told about the storming of the Bastille?   42

4 Royal Blood

What made the revolutionaries kill the King?   66

5 **Terror!**

Why do people still argue about   82
Robespierre?

6 **Citoyennes**

What did the French Revolution   96
mean for women?

7 **'Bonaparte – my hero!'**

What was Napoleon's greatest   112
artist trying to tell us?

8 **'If only, if only…'**

Why was Napoleon finally   124
defeated at Waterloo?

9 **'So what?'**

What has studying the French   142
Revolution done for you?

'The blood you are to shed...'

At five o'clock on the morning of 21 January 1793, Louis XVI King of France was woken by one of his servants. The King dressed in simple clothes and attended Mass. Outside, he heard the rhythmic beating of drums. Louis said, calmly, "I expect it's the National Guard beginning to assemble". He sat by the stove in his room and waited. At around eight o'clock the soldiers arrived. The King asked them if his servant could cut his hair to spare him the humiliation of having his hair cropped on the scaffold. They refused.

The King walked to the waiting green carriage. He turned once or twice towards the tower as if to say goodbye. For two hours, the King's carriage made its way through the streets of Paris to the *Place de la Revolution*. It was a damp, foggy morning, but thousands of people lined the streets. They waited silently. In front of the carriage marched the drummers and line after line of National Guardsmen with muskets and pikes on their shoulders. The revolutionaries were taking no chances.

At ten o'clock the procession arrived at the scaffold. Charles Sanson, the executioner, and his assistants, cut off the hair which grew over the King's neck. They tied Louis' hands behind his back. The King walked across the platform, and tried to address his people: "I die innocent of all the crimes of which I have been charged. I pardon those who have brought about my death and I pray that the blood you are about to shed may never be required of France ..." At that moment a roll of drums drowned out whatever else the King was about to say.

Sanson and his assistants strapped Louis face down on the plank of the guillotine. The blade hissed down. The king let out a terrible scream. His head was not severed by the first blow because his neck was too fat. When it finally fell into the basket, the executioner pulled the head out and showed it dripping with blood to the people.

The King's head was placed between his legs and the body was taken to a cemetery in Paris. It was placed in a plain wooden coffin used for the poorest of funerals. The coffin was buried in a grave said to be ten feet deep.

Think

● In what ways did the revolutionaries show a lack of respect for Louis XVI on the day of his execution?

The revolution that led to the execution of King Louis XVI was one of the most important events in history. During the 1780s France – one of Europe's most powerful countries – reached a crisis. From 1789 the people of France were caught up in a violent revolution. This book will help you to understand what went wrong in France, what happened during the Revolution, and what became of the citizens of France. It is quite a story.

The blood of the murdered crying for vengeance, the execution of Louis XVI by James Gillray, late eighteenth-century

High hopes and big complaints

What was everyone complaining about in 1789?

Human beings are always complaining. Imagine what would happen if instead of being told to "stop complaining", you were actually *invited* to write down all your complaints. This is what happened in 1789, in France. And in France, there was plenty to complain about.

1789 was an exciting and important moment for people all over France. In the spring, there were **elections**. Those people who were allowed to vote chose **deputies** to represent them in a huge gathering called the **Estates General**. No one alive in France at that time would have been able to remember an Estates General. The Estates General had not met for 175 years.

The people were invited to write down all their complaints so that the Estates General could discuss them. They were asked to draw up special notebooks of complaints or ***cahiers de doléances***. The King said that he had called the Estates General, "not only that the Estates might give their advice on everything we shall ask them to discuss, but also that they may tell us the wishes and grievances of our people so that every kind of abuse will be reformed."

That was a very big promise. Hopes were high all over France. Many of these complaints had been brewing for a long time.

Over 60,000 *cahiers* were drawn up. Here is part of just one *cahier*. It was drawn up by a village in northern France. You will find some of the complaints puzzling:

Cahier de doléance
St Germain sous Cailly, District of Rouen.
Population: 57 families.

1 We want an end to all taxes and tolls at town gates and their replacement by a single tax.

2 We want tax-free salt.

3 We want to end begging. Each parish should pay for the relief of poor people's suffering.

4 We want to end the right of the mill.

5 The nobles should have to pay the *taille* (a tax on land or income) and the *capitation* (a poll tax).

7 We want the amount we pay as a *tithe* (a tenth of yearly income paid to the church) to be adjusted.

8 We want a new way of maintaining the roads. It is most unfair that poor people and others who do not have carriages have to contribute to the upkeep of roads that they never use. It would be fairer if the clergy and the nobles had to pay for it.

9 We want to end compulsory service in the army. It deprives workers, old people and the ill of young men on whom they depend.

10 We want the right to kill crows.

13 We want the destruction of all rabbit warrens.

14 We want the pigeons to be kept in the dovecote from July to November.

15 We want controls on the price of bread.

Think

- Think of some possible reasons why the villagers might have been so bothered about crows, rabbits and pigeons.

- How would you sum up what most of these complaints seem to be about? See if you can work out any connections or themes.

Your enquiry

Historians need knowledge to understand sources like the *cahiers de doleances*. By the end of this enquiry you will have enough knowledge to understand exactly why the villages such as St Germain sous Cailly complained in the way they did.

You will also understand different complaints made by other French people, and other ways of complaining. You will be able to see what these complaints tell us about France's problems at this time.

At the end of the enquiry, you will use that knowledge to place this *cahier* in context.

Complaining about privileges and rights

Divided by birth and wealth

There were 28 million people living in France in 1789. Nearly all of them fitted into one of four main social groups.

The nobility

This is the Duke of Penthièvre. He and his family are drinking a new, fashionable drink – chocolate. The nobility were the ruling class. They owned land. They also did all the important and well-paid jobs in the King's government. The nobility had titles such as Duke, Marquis, Count or Viscount. This made them seem very different from the common people.

About 350,000 French people were nobles. They owned about 25% of the land.

The Duke of Penthievre, a painting by Jean Baptiste Charpentier, 1768

The bourgeoisie

This family certainly had plenty of money. Many of the *bourgeoisie* were educated and well-off. But they did not have any titles or special privileges because they were not members of the nobility. They made their money from the professions and from trade. *Bourgeoisie* included doctors, lawyers, office holders, bankers, traders, teachers, artists and some master craftsmen. The family in the picture were ship-owners. They were the Gohin family and they lived in Rouen.

The Gohin family, a painting by Louis Leopold Boilly, 1787

About two and a half million people belonged to the *bourgeoisie*. They owned about 30% of the land.

Think

- These four groups were very unequal in numbers. In what other ways were they unequal?

- Which complaints in the *cahier* on page 7 do these two pages help to explain?

- Looking at the information on the bourgeoisie, what kinds of things do you think that they might have complained about?

Sieur Jadot's joinery workshop, an eighteenth-century French engraving

The town workers

These French people are town workers. They are working in a carpenter's workshop. The towns were full of shopkeepers, traders, craftsmen, builders or labourers. Some of these people were quite independent and highly skilled, owning small shops or workshops and making a reasonable living. Some were manual labourers who were often struggling, especially if wages fell or the price of bread went up. There were also unemployed people in the towns and plenty of beggars. At times of bad harvests, the numbers of unemployed people in Paris swelled as desperate people came in from the countryside hoping for work or cheaper food.

About two million people worked in the towns. Very few owned any land.

The peasants

These French people are peasants. Peasants lived in the countryside and farmed the land. Together, the peasants owned about a quarter of the land of France. At the top were richer, landowning peasantry and tenant farmers. At the bottom were the *journaliers* or day labourers who could never be sure where the next day's work would come from. Peasants also had to do a number of days work for their local lord, without any pay.

About 22 million French people were peasants. The peasants owned about 35% of the land.

A busy harvesting scene by Le Sieur Liger, 1723

Divided by law: the three estates

French society was divided up in an other way, too. According to French law, all people were members of one of three **estates**.

In the **First Estate** were the clergy. These people had the highest position in society. The Catholic Church controlled the daily lives of almost everyone in France. It controlled education. It provided care for the sick. The clergy of the First Estate had many special privileges: they did not have to do military service and they could only be tried in their own law courts. The Church as a whole was very wealthy. But there was a big difference in wealth and power between the bishops, archbishops and cardinals – who came from the nobility – and the humble parish priests who were sometimes very poor.
There were about 130,000 people in the First Estate.

In the **Second Estate** were the nobility. The **nobility of the sword** were ancient families who gained their position by birth. They were princes of royal blood. The **nobility of the robe** gained their noble status from the work that they did, performing a special job such as being a judge or doing some work for the government. You could even buy these special jobs from the King. The nobility had many privileges. They did not have to pay many taxes.
There were about 350,000 people in the Second Estate.

In the **Third Estate** was everybody else. This was a very mixed group of people. The vast majority were peasants, making up about 80-90% of the population. The rest were urban workers and bourgeoisie. The third estate had no privileges.
There were about 27 million in the Third Estate.

We can tell that people were complaining by looking at pictures and writings made at the time. This picture shows what some people thought of the system of the three estates.

The Game Must End Soon, an eighteenth-century French engraving

Think

- Work out who belonged to which estate in this picture.

- What point do you think the artist is trying to make?

- What does the caption suggest about people's hopes at the time?

This system seemed very unfair. Once, the system might have made sense. Back in the middle ages, the three estates were very important in making French society work. Nobles were originally soldiers who fought for France in wartime. The clergy ran the country's education and religious life. In return for this important work, the king had given the nobles and clergy their own estates and privileges.

By 1789, however, the nobles and clergy were less important. Other people went to war, not just the nobles. The system was outdated and the complaints were growing.

What made the system seem really unfair was the fact that the nobles and the clergy hardly had to pay any tax! Even when they did pay tax, they paid no more than the poorest people.

This chart shows you just how unfair things had become:

	Tax name	Type of tax	Who paid?	Who did not have to pay?
Direct taxes	*Taille*	tax on land or income	all citizens	nobles, clergy
	Capitation	poll tax	all citizens	nobody, but many nobles and clergy got out of paying.
	Twentieths	income tax	all citizens	nobody, but many nobles and clergy got out of paying.
	Corvée	labour tax, requiring unpaid work mending royal roads	all able-bodied men	nobles, clergy, townspeople, postmasters, school teachers, shepherds
Indirect taxes	*Gabelle*	tax on salt	anybody buying salt	people living in four provinces
	Octroi	tax paid at the town gates, on goods being taken to market	the traders who transported the goods	nobody

Think

- Which of the complaints in the *cahier* on page 7 now make more sense?

This cartoon from the 1780s shows what some people thought about taxes, rights and dues. On the rock is written *Taille*, *Impots* (dues) and *Corvée*.

All that was quite enough to complain about. But there was more, especially for the peasants in the countryside. As well as paying taxes to the government, millions of peasants had to pay money to their landlords. As tenants on the land, the peasants owed special dues to their landlords. The chart on page 13 shows some of these **feudal** rights and dues.

The Third Estate under the tax burden, an eighteenth-century French engraving

Some of the feudal rights and dues that peasants had to pay.

Rights	The right of the oven	Peasants had to bake their bread in an oven owned by the landlord, paying a fee to use it.
	The right of the mill	Peasants had to grind corn in the landlord's windmill or watermill, and pay for it.
	The right of the hunt	The landlord could ride over his tenants' crops while hunting.
	The right of the warren	The landlord could keep rabbits. Tenants could not kill them, even when they damaged their crops.
	The right of the dovecote	The landlord could keep pigeons. Tenants could not kill them, even when they damaged their crops.
Dues	The *corvée*	Peasants had to do several days' unpaid work for the landlord each year.
	The *cens*	Peasants had to pay tax to the landlord each year.
	The *champart*	Peasants had to give the landlord a portion of the crops each year.

Think

- Who are the people standing on the rock?

- What message is the cartoonist trying to get across?

- Which of the complaints in the *cahier* on page 7 now make more sense?

STEP 1

Think about what a male peasant living in rural France might have wanted to complain about. He has to struggle to feed his family. He has been invited to a meeting to share what he thinks are his main problems, but he hasn't much time! He will only be allowed to speak for a minute. In just three sentences he must explain what is wrong with France. What does he see are the causes of his problems? Write a speech bubble for him. Begin your sentences with 'The trouble with France...'. Then, in another three sentences, he must say what he would like to happen. What changes does he think should be made? What does he want?

The trouble with France...

I want...

13

Complaining about the price of bread

The importance of a loaf

Many French people lived in terrible poverty. This eighteenth-century writer described the conditions of many workers in Paris. One family, he said,

> "... lives in a single room, in which the four walls are bare, the beds have no covers. All the furniture together is not worth twenty crowns*. Every three months, the inhabitants are thrown out for owing back rent and must find another hole to live in. Thus, they wander, taking their miserable possessions from refuge to refuge."

Louis-Sebastien Mercier, Tableau de Paris, 1783.

* about £120 in present day prices

But it was not just the desperately poor, unemployed and destitute who had something to complain about. Throughout the 1780s the ordinary wage-earning worker, the skilled craftsman and the shopkeeper were at risk from bread prices shooting up.

Imagine a working, wage-earning family of five living in Paris. After they had paid for absolute essentials – such as rent of a single room, clothing, heating, soap, candles or lamp oil, and, of course paid their taxes – they would have had about 13 sous a day left for food.

What could you buy with 13 sous? Not very much. As long as prices did not get too high and wages did not fall, you could cope, but few families would have had much money left over after buying bread, as these prices show:

Here are some typical prices in Paris in August 1788.

> Bread (loaf) - 9 sous
> Mutton (per pound) – 14 sous
> Butter (per pound) – 14 sous
> Eggs (per 10) – 8 sous
> Beef (per pound) 11 sous

*Very roughly, one sou is about 10 pence in today's money.

For our family of five, meat was a rare treat even in the good times. Bread was what mattered. Our family of five would have needed a loaf a day.

Think

Now you can see why the price of a loaf mattered. If the price of bread rose to 14 sous, what do you think would have been the consequences of each of these options open to them?

- Buy no firewood, candles or soap for several months?
- Pay no taxes?
- Save stale bread and eat only a tiny morsel a day?
- Steal?
- Starve?
- Borrow money?

The importance of the weather

In the 1780s there were terrible harvests. This was disastrous for almost everyone.

Think about what a bad harvest would mean for different people in France. This flow-chart shows you what would have happened:

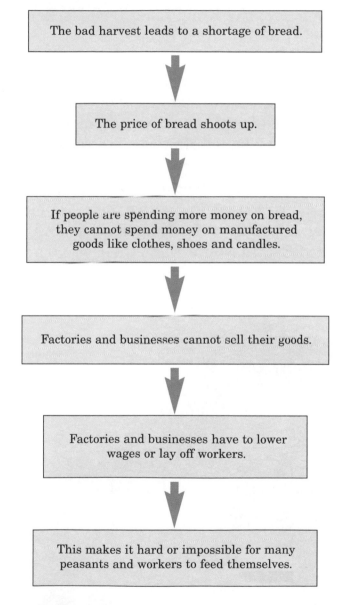

So just at the time when both peasants and workers need employment **more than ever before** (to pay for all that expensive bread), unemployment was getting much worse.

France then faced a **terrible disaster**. On 13 July 1788, a massive hailstorm destroyed cornfields, vineyards and orchards all over France. Then there was no rain at all and the land dried out. It was the worst harvest anyone had ever known. This was followed by the coldest winter anyone had ever known. Rivers froze over, stopping watermills from grinding flour. When the snow thawed in the spring, floods ruined the farmland.

By March 1789, the price of bread had risen to 14 sous per loaf. At times it hit 15 sous. By the spring of 1789 a poor family in Paris could be spending 88% of all their earnings on bread. Those that had lost their jobs were likely to starve.

Many peasant communities in the countryside complained about these things in the *cahiers*. Small landowners and labourers managed to complain about the price of bread. In Rouen, the price of bread rose to 16 sous in 1789 and the peasants used their *cahier* to demand that it be reduced by half. Even the voice of the landless labourer was heard in some of the cahiers from the countryside.

Meanwhile, in the towns, however, we hardly hear the voice of the poorest labourers and wage-earners. They did not usually get heard when the *cahiers* of the Third Estate were drawn up.

But there were other ways of making yourself heard. There were other ways of complaining loudly, such as riots and strikes. The most famous and important of these riots were the Réveillon riots.

15

Complaining on the streets: The Réveillon riots

Monsieur Réveillon had a very good reputation with his 350 workers. He paid his workers 25 sous a day when most other factory owners only paid 20. On 23 April 1789, Monsieur Réveillon made a speech. He spoke about the problems of trying to run a factory when the costs were so high. He called for the price of bread to go down so that it would be possible to pay lower wages.

Réveillon probably *did* want the price of bread to go down. But the workers on the streets only heard the bit about the wages. Workers in a part of Paris called the *Faubourg St Antoine* were furious. On 28 April, they attacked Réveillon's house and factory. They also attacked the house of another manufacturer – the owner of a powder factory called Henriot. They broke into his house and destroyed all his furniture.

The riots carried on the next day spreading to many other workers. No work was done in the factories and docks that day. At least 50 people were killed or wounded by the troops who were sent out to disperse them.

This riot tells us what the people were *really* angry about – and it was mainly the price of bread. The fear that wages would go down was enough to push people over the edge. As the crowds dispersed they tried to break into two food shops. Clearly, it was bread that mattered.

What the rioters **did** also helps us to work out what the rioters **thought**. Their actions show us who the rioters thought were to blame. They did not blame the King. In fact, quite the opposite. As they rioted, they shouted:

"Long Live the King! Long Live Necker! Long Live the Third Estate!"

The rioters were hopeful because the Third Estate was about to meet in the Estates General (it was due to meet in May). They hoped that the Third Estate would champion them and that the King and his minister Necker would support the Third Estate in ending their troubles. They hoped that the King, Necker and the Third Estate would right their wrongs and provide cheap, plentiful bread.

The Reveillon Riot of April 1789, an eighteenth-century French engraving

So if they did not blame the King, who did they blame? They blamed all sorts of other people.

- Some blamed wealthy landowners and grain merchants. They accused them of hoarding grain to keep prices high.

- Some blamed the customs posts outside the city where anyone transporting grain had to pay high duties, pushing prices up.

- Some blamed the factory owners and manufacters for laying off workers and not paying high wages.

Angry crowds also took other action to make their complaints known and to try to get what they wanted. For example, they attacked convoys of grain. Later, they attacked the customs posts around the city.

We know that many small traders and discontented workers took part in the riots – not just the poorest and starving. All these people felt that they were being treated unjustly.

STEP 2

Think about the complaints of a group of different people in Paris in April 1789, just a week before the Estates General met:

- A wage-earner who has just been made unemployed by his factory and has no money to buy bread for his family.

- A factory worker in a job who has barely enough money to buy bread and who is very worried that the prices might get even higher and wages even lower.

- A small shopkeeper selling candles and lamp-oil.

- A skilled craftsman making hats who is angry that merchants are now paying much less for his hats.

These people are all slightly different, but they have something in common to complain about – the price of bread. Imagine that they are complaining loudly in the streets about their problems. Between all four of them, they only have six sentences. In just three sentences explain, from their point of view, what is wrong with France in 1789. What do they see as the causes of their problems? Who will they blame? Begin your sentences with 'The trouble with France...'. Then, in another three sentences, say what they would like to happen. What do they hope for? What would they like to see done? What would they like the deputies at the Third Estate to argue for? What changes would they like to see made? What do they want? Your four people might not normally agree with each other but this time, they do.

The trouble with France...

We want...

17

Complaining about laws and government

Power unlimited?

There were other kinds of complaint, too. Different sorts of people had been complaining for a some time about how France was run. This kind of complaint was about power, especially the power held by the King.

Many people were concerned that there were very few **limits** on Louis' power. For example, if Louis wanted to imprison anyone, all he had to do was send a *lettre de cachet*. This means 'sealed letter'. A person whose name appeared on that letter could be sent into exile or put in prison, without a trial. The King's ministers were free to use these letters. During Louis XVI's reign, about 14,000 sealed letters were sent.

In 1770, some Paris lawyers wrote to the King, complaining,

Louis XVI in Coronation Robes, a painting by Joseph Siffred Duplessis, about 1774

"These orders signed by your Majesty are full of names that Your Majesty can never have known. They are there because your ministers have put them there. None of your subjects is safe."

If we compare the power of Louis XVI with the power of the King of England, George III, there is a big difference. George III had his power limited by a parliament. Louis XVI, however, had **absolute authority**. He was not responsible to a parliament. He said that he was responsible only to God.

France did have 13 **parlements** but don't confuse these with the British **parliament**. The French parlements were just law-courts. Only nobles sat in them. The Paris Parlement was the most important. Parlements were allowed to criticise the King but the King was allowed to ignore them.

It was also possible to hold a special meeting of elected **representatives** of each of the three estates. This was called the **Estates General**. But only the King could call an Estates General and the last time one had met was in 1614!

No wonder Louis said, in 1766,

"sovereign power belongs to me alone – it is not dependent on or shared with anyone else".

Of course, Louis was not *completely* free to do *exactly* has he liked. He still had to honour customs and laws. And he could not interfere with the rights and privileges of special, independent bodies like the Assembly of the Clergy. But compared with English kings, he could mostly do as he pleased.

Louis did have ministers to advise him. He gave them power but he did not have to listen to them. The **Controller-General**, in charge of finances, was the most important minister. But there was no **cabinet**, where ministers could meet together. Each minister dealt with the King individually.

In the 1780s and 90s, more and more people began to criticise Louis's power. By 1789, many were criticising the whole system of government, laws and institutions in France. We call that system the ***ancien regime***.

Think

- Louis did not have a special minister called a Prime Minister. Why do you think that he would not want one?

- How was the power of kings in France different from the power of kings in Britain?

- Why might it have been dangerous for the King to have so much power?

The Orangery at Versailles, a painting by Pierre-Denis Martin, early eighteenth-century

Louis governed France with the help of hundreds of nobles who lived with him at Versailles in this enormous palace.

The Austrian woman

By the 1780s there was another reason why Louis was becoming unpopular. The problem was his wife ...

Queen Marie Antoinette was Austrian. People on the streets called her the 'Austrian Woman' – *Autrichienne*. This was a way of being rude about her. *Chienne*, in French, means 'bitch'.

Marie Antoinette was disliked for:
- being foreign;
- spending lots of money on clothes, jewellery and gambling;
- having favourites at court;
- being unfaithful to Louis (or so many people said...)

Complaints from the philosophes

A group of educated people led some of these criticisms about the government of France and royal power. These people were called *philosophes*. They were writers, journalists and scientists. They shared a way of thinking that was growing in the eighteenth century. We call this way of thinking and the ideas that came out of it, the **Enlightenment**.

Enlightenment thinkers believed that it was possible to create a much better, or even perfect society. They believed that society should not stay the same just because of tradition had always made it that way. For the *philosophes*, tradition was not a good reason for keeping things as they were. Everything should be tested and questioned. Everything should be based on reason, not tradition.

Here are two very famous *philosophes*:

Jean-Jacques Rousseau (1712-78)

Rousseau developed some very important ideas from the Enlightenment. One of these was the 'social contract'. He believed that more people should take part in government, and that government and people should serve each other. He also used words from the ancient, classical world, like 'citizen'. He believed that it was the citizens of a country who made up the nation. These citizens had both duties and rights. He wanted general assemblies where the government would learn ordinary people's wishes.

François-Marie Voltaire (1694-1778)

Voltaire complained about many wrongs in French society. He complained about injustice in the law and about the power and beliefs of the French Church. He believed that non-Catholics should be tolerated and so he campaigned for religious freedom. Above all, he complained about the cruel laws and cruel punishments that were still used in France.

This picture shows the kind of punishment that Voltaire was complaining about. It shows a man being 'broken on a wheel'. This means that he was tied to a cartwheel and his legs and arms were smashed with an iron bar. It was an agonising, slow death. Later, the victim would be strangled and his body burned.

The *philosophes* wanted more freedoms for people to speak, write and act. These freedoms did not exist in France in the eighteenth century. They wanted things like freedom of the press, freedom of speech, freedom of trade, freedom from imprisonment without trial. They did not expect all people to be equal, but they did want everyone to be treated fairly. Most did not want to get rid of the monarchy (except Rousseau, who did).

The *philosophes* were writers. Their books and pamphlets reached many educated people in towns all over France. By 1789, they would have reached only very few ordinary people, however. In the Third Estate, only the educated and better-off people would have come across these books and pamphlets.

We know that many nobles read the writings of Rousseau, Voltaire and the other *philosophes*. Many noblemen thought that the King had too much power. They wanted an assembly to have the right to vote taxes and pass laws. But they did not want the Third Estate to get too powerful instead! Many nobles only wanted nobles in such an assembly.

Nevertheless, what the noblemen of the Second Estate wrote in many of their *cahiers* might surprise you. About 90% of the *cahiers* written by the nobles, show that they were ready to give up some of their special privileges. It was not just the people of the Third Estate who wanted changes in France.

Such nobles attacked the King and his ministers for having too much power. They did not want a completely equal society but they did want to see some changes in the way France was governed. **They wanted to see the King's power limited**.

STEP 3

This time our complainer is an educated, liberal nobleman. This nobleman reads the writings of Voltaire. He does not want to get rid of the King (he thinks Rousseau goes a bit too far). He thinks that the King and many of his ministers should have to listen to the important people of the land and take advice from them.

He is talking to some friends of his after dinner one evening. What will he say? Fill in his speech bubbles:

One very big complaint from the Third Estate

The complaints that the three different estates made in their *cahiers* had one big thing in common. The three estates were all against the King having so much power. They all wanted a king whose powers would be limited by an elected assembly. They all agreed that an assembly should have the right to vote taxes and pass laws.

But there was **one great big issue** on which the Third Estate was different from the First and Second Estates. This is going to become very important in our story...

When the Estates General last met in 1614, the three estates had each met separately. Each estate was granted one vote only and that was how decisions were made.

Think

● If each estate had only one vote, what would have happened every time the Third Estate disagreed with the First and Second Estates?

But in 1789, the Third Estate was not going to have this. It would mean that the Third Estate would always be outvoted by the First and Second!

Instead, the Third Estate wanted voting by 'head'. They also thought that the Third Estate should have twice as many votes as each of the other estates as it was so much bigger. The Third Estate knew that if they got their way over these things, they would be able to make decisions.

The nobility did not want this. They tried to stop it and there were lots of debates about it in 1788. The Third Estate was furious. In January 1789, Abbé Sieyès wrote a pamphlet entitled, *What is the Third Estate?* In it, he said that the Third Estate was 'everything'.

The Third Estate was asking for big trouble, from the King, from the churchmen in the First Estate and from the nobles in the Second Estate.

Think about a lawyer in the Third Estate. He has been elected to the Estates General. He agrees with Abbé Sieyès. He agrees with Rousseau. He is worried about unfair laws. He is worried about the King having too much powers. Look over pages 18 to 24 and work out what he might be complaining about. What does he want? Fill in a speech bubble for him, as you did in previous STEPS: 'The trouble with France is … ' and 'I want …'

Thinking your enquiry through

You will now understand all the complaints in the *cahier* on page 7. You will also know about many other kinds of complaints. The people complaining came from very different backgrounds. Sometimes they complained about very different things, sometimes about exactly the same thing. It depended on who they were, what they had experienced and what ideas they had come across.

Using the work you have done on your Steps, fill in a copy of this chart. You will need a very large piece of paper. This activity will show how well you can apply your new knowledge to understanding one source. It will also show what you understand about other kinds of complaints from different kinds of people. You will then be placing your source **in context**.

What the cahier tells me about <u>who</u> was complaining	What the cahier tells me about <u>why</u> they were complaining.
Your teacher will give you a copy of the *cahier* on page 7 to put here.	
Different sorts of complaints <u>not</u> found in this *cahier* but likely to be found in others.	The kinds of people who would have been making those complaints.

'We will only leave at the point of bayonets.'

What's the story behind the Tennis Court Oath?

The Tennis Court Oath, 20th June 1789, a painting based on the detailed drawing by Jacques Louis David in 1791

Think

- Which of these words describe the people in the picture: determined, worried, relaxed, excited, united, confused, hopeful, expectant, triumphant, defeated?

- What kinds of people can you see in the picture? Are they mostly bourgeoisie? mostly nobles? mostly poor peasants? can you find any clergymen?

This painting shows nearly 600 people holding an important meeting in a most unusual place. They are all in an indoor tennis court in the grounds of the King's palace at Versailles. In the picture there are 577 deputies from the Third Estate. Nearly all of these were from the bourgeoisie. They have also been joined by seven clergymen. All these people had been elected to attend the meeting of the Estates General, called for 5 May 1789.

The painting shows something that happened on 20 June, six weeks **after** the Estates General first met. Trying to escape from pouring rain, these people found themselves rushing into the nearest empty building. There they swore an oath to carry on meeting until they had changed the way France was governed. This is what you can see in the painting. The man in the centre, standing on a table, is swearing an oath. French people later called this the Tennis Court Oath.

Without knowing the story behind it, this is a very puzzling event. It throws up lots of questions: Why didn't these deputies of the Third Estate have anywhere to meet? Why had seven clergymen joined them? Where were the other clergy? Where were the nobles? What on earth had they been doing for six weeks since the Estates General first met? Why did they want to swear an oath?

To answer these questions, we need to know the story that **lies behind** this event. We need to discover the story that led up to the Tennis Court Oath.

Your enquiry

We are *not going to tell you* the story. We are just going to give you the facts. **You** are going to tell the story. You are going to weave the facts together to make a proper historical narrative.

A good historical narrative needs to be accurate and to include the relevant facts. But sometimes it is difficult to decide which facts to use and where to share them with your reader. A historical narrative also needs to be fascinating to read. The reader must want to go on reading.

By the end of this enquiry you will have written the story of the three years before the French Revolution. You will need to make choices about the order in which you will tell things to your reader, how you will share new material in an interesting way and how you will show the importance of these events.

The first part of the story is written for you. In Step 1 you will look back at our writing and to pick out all the features of good historical narrative that you can find. In Steps 2, 3 and 4, you will write the rest of the narrative yourselves.

Part One: An Assembly of Notables defies the King

In 1786, Louis XVI had very big problems. The worst problems of all were to do with money. This chart shows just how bad his money problems were.

The King was spending much more than his income. This is called a **deficit**.

Think

- What kinds of things did the French government spend money on?

- How can you tell from the chart that the French government had borrowed a lot of money?

- Do you think that the French government could have cut its spending? If so, how?

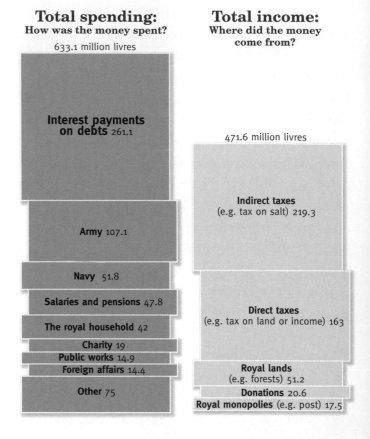

Total spending:
How was the money spent?
633.1 million livres

Interest payments on debts 261.1

Army 107.1

Navy 51.8

Salaries and pensions 47.8

The royal household 42

Charity 19

Public works 14.9

Foreign affairs 14.4

Other 75

Total income:
Where did the money come from?

471.6 million livres

Indirect taxes
(e.g. tax on salt) 219.3

Direct taxes
(e.g. tax on land or income) 163

Royal lands
(e.g. forests) 51.2

Donations 20.6

Royal monopolies (e.g. post) 17.5

Louis XVI had a special minister in charge of **finances**. He was called Calonne. Early in 1786 Calonne went to see the King. Calonne was **always** going to see the King. This time, however, he had a firm message. If something were not done quickly, the French government would go bankrupt. The King had three options. He could borrow more money. He could cut spending. He could increase taxes.

The first option was crazy. The second was impossible. Only the third – raising taxes – could make any difference. And even this was a problem. It was impossible to tax the ordinary people much more. The King needed to raise taxes from the wealthy, those that owned land. But the nobles and the clergy had a tradition of not paying many taxes. So this was going to be very difficult indeed.

Calonne talked to the King. He was a good talker. With his lace cuffs and his gold-topped cane, we can picture him charming and persuading the King. The King was impressed by him.

Calonne could be reckless and bold. He had a dreadful temper when he did not get his own way.

Confident that he could persuade the King, Calonne made a plan. He decided that drastic action was necessary. There was only one thing for it: the King would have to change the tax system. Calonne decided to introduce a new tax on land which all landowners would have to pay.

Calonne knew that the landowners would hate this. He also knew that the landowners could easily stop it from happening. All new laws had to be registered in the Paris **Parlement**. And who controlled the Parlement? The landowners.

Other finance ministers like Turgot and Necker had tried to tax the rich before and got nowhere. No matter how often they tried, they never succeeded. But Calonne was more cunning. He did something that other finance ministers had not tried. Calonne invited 150 important nobles and clergymen to come to Paris and form a special **Assembly** of **Notables**. He wanted this assembly to approve the new tax. Calonne's clever move was to make sure that he only invited loyal supporters of the king.

But Calonne's clever move was not clever enough. When the Assembly of Notables met in February 1787, it still refused to agree the new taxes. The members of the Assembly said that they did not have the power to approve new taxes. They were not going to help. They said that the King would just have to call the **Estates General**.

Calonne's plan had failed. On April 8th 1787, Louis dismissed him. Then he **exiled** Calonne from Paris. Perhaps the King was foolish. Perhaps if he had really backed Calonne, it might have saved the monarchy. But Louis was indecisive. It seems as though he did not know what he wanted. He still did not know what to do for the best.

When Louis exiled Calonne, the people of Paris celebrated. They lit bonfires. They threw little fireworks in the faces of the King's soldiers. They even made a model of Calonne. They called it 'Monsieur Deficit'. They carried it to a large square in the centre of Paris and burned it.

29

Look back over the story on pages 28 and 29. Find an example of each of the following:

a) Deliberate repetition. For example, *did not know* appears twice in one paragraph. *Perhaps* is repeated in one paragraph. Find another example of this kind of repetition.

b) Short crisp sentences at the starts of paragraphs.

c) Punchy, surprising, or thought-provoking sentences at the ends of paragraphs.

d) Adverbs such as *even...*, or *still...* and adverbial phrases such as, *no matter how often...* to emphasise the seriousness of the situation.

e) Highlighting contrasts, surprises and turnarounds for the reader using connectives like *but* and *however*. You can create different effects with these words, depending on whether you use them at the beginning or in the middle of sentences.

f) Linking two events, using a sentence that begins with *When....,*. We have put one of these sentences in green. Find the other one. Which two events does it link?

g) Weaving in of background information. Such information is not part of the events in the story but it is necessary to help the reader to understand those events. There is one example in red. Find some others. The challenge is to do this 'weaving in' without spoiling the flow of the story.

h) Weaving in tiny details. There are little details in this story that seem tiny and unimportant. Perhaps we do not need them. But they help the reader to get interested in characters or events. For example, we read about Calonne's bad temper. Find other examples of small details. What is the author trying to suggest by including such odd little details in the story?

i) Direct comments by the narrator. Sometimes, we have added in our own direct comments by describing a character as clever or cunning. Sometimes we have commented on events, saying what might have happened if things had been different. Here we have used *Perhaps…* . Find all the places where we, the authors, seem to be sharing our own views or opinions.

j) Suspense and punch at the end. How does the final paragraph make the reader start to guess at what might happen next?

Now, over to you...

You are now going to finish this narrative by writing three more sections, one in each 'Step'. These sections will be called.

The Paris Parlement defies the King

The Third Estate defies the King

The National Assembly defies the King

Your last section will take you right up to the events leading to the Tennis Court Oath and your story will be complete.

In each Step you will be given the following information:

- main facts to shape your narrative;
- things happening elsewhere at the same time (for you to weave in);
- background information (for you to weave in *if* you think the reader needs it);
- smaller details to make your narrative more interesting, vivid or powerful.

Part Two: The Paris Parlement defies the king

Main facts to shape your narrative

Below, you will find a list of events and developments for your story. We have presented them in the right order but in a boring way. Your job is to link these main facts together so that they sound like a story. You are going to help the reader to see how these events are **connected.**

This is how you can go about it:

- **Re-word** our facts so that they are in the past tense.

- Decide how to **group** the facts together to make three or four paragraphs.

- Use plenty of **linking words**, both at the beginning of sentences and in the middle of sentences:

    words to show consequences: *As a result.. And so... Not surprisingly...*

    words to show contrasts and surprises: *...however... but...*

    words to emphasise how things keep repeating themselves: *Once again... Yet again...For the second time...*

    using the word 'When' at the start of a sentence to show how one thing happening triggered another thing happening. For example, you could link two of the facts below by rewriting them like this: *When Louis exiled the*

Parlement from Paris, angry protests took place all over France.

- Include some **short punchy sentences**.

- Think carefully about the **beginnings and endings of paragraphs**. Can you create a sense of drama at the end of a paragraph with a short sentence?

- Add in some **comment** of your own. What do you think of Louis? You could use words like *cunning*, *clever*, *foolish* or you could comment on how things might have been different (Louis could have...Louis should have...? Perhaps, if Louis ..., ...)

All the facts below are in the right order. You just have to weave them together so that they flow better, so that they feel like a story.

Here are your main facts:

Louis appoints a new minister called Brienne.

(25 May 1787) Louis dismisses the Assembly of Notables.

Louis and Brienne try to introduce the new tax.

The nobles in the Paris Parlement refuse to register the new tax.

The Paris Parlement says that the only the Estates General has the power to approve taxes.

Louis is furious. He exiles the Parlement from Paris. (15 August 1787)

(September 1787) Louis cannot get any money without the Parlement. He gives in. He allows the Parlement to come back to Paris.

(November 1787) The King tries to force the Paris Parlement to agree to some loans. He surrounds it with troops. He fails.

(3 May 1788) The Paris Parlement proclaims some "fundamental laws": 1) Only the Estates General can vote for taxes; 2) No Frenchman can be imprisoned without trial.

Louis is furious. Using a royal edict, he tries to take away the rights of *all* the parlements to register taxes.

The nobles are furious. They encourage protests and riots all over France. This "Revolt of the Nobles" lasts several months.

(August 1788) The royal treasury is empty. Louis gives in. He orders elections for an Estates General. Brienne resigns. The King replaces him with Necker.

Things happening elsewhere, at the same time

Important developments were happening at the same time as the events listed above. You must decide **where** you are going to weave these into your narrative.

Here are two, separate things that were happening elsewhere, for you to weave in:

Between May and September 1788 there are riots and disturbances in many parts of France. There are some particularly violent riots in Grenobles and Rennes in June.

Mass hunger is growing in the countryside. On 13 July 1788 a massive hailstorm destroys cornfields, vegetable plots, orchards and vineyards. There is then a terrible drought. The harvest of 1788 is very poor.

You must also decide how you are going to weave in these other developments. You could use words like *Meanwhile... At the same time...* to show that they were occurring at the same time.

Background information

Your reader needs to know about this thing called an **Estates General**.

You already know this from the last enquiry. But your reader might not!

Remind yourself of some basic facts about the three estates on pages 10 to 11. Then look up the information about the **Estates General** on pages 18 and 23.

Think about where you might need to weave this information into your story. Remember, you don't want to interrupt your story too much, or you will make it dull! Equally, your reader must not become confused when the **Estates General** is mentioned. So you must decide just how much you need to say to help your reader.

Smaller details

You now need smaller details to make your narrative catch your reader's imagination. You want to help your readers to 'see' or to visualise the events in their own minds.

Here is one extra detail. Decide where it fits into your story. Into which paragraph will you put it? How can you use this detail to interest the reader?

> In Grenoble on 7 June 1788, one of the riots becomes very violent. Protesters climb onto the rooftops and pelt soldiers with tiles. People start to call this day the Day of Tiles.

The Day of the Tiles in Grenoble, 7 June 1788, painted by Alexander Debelle, one hundred years later. You cannot put this painting into your narrative but, having seen it, how could you help your readers to 'see' this event as they read'?

Part Three: The Third Estate defies the King

Main facts to shape your narrative

Here is a list of events and developments to shape the next stage of your narrative. Link these main facts together so that they sound like a story.

Choose language that helps the reader to see how these events are connected, just as you did in Step 2. Look again at page 32.

Here are your main facts:

In September 1788, the Third Estate complains that the voting system of the Estates General is unfair.

The Third Estate asks the King to double its numbers. It also asks for its members to have one vote each.

By December 1788 the government is completely bankrupt. The new finance minister, Necker, advises the King to give in to the Third Estate.

In December 1788 the King gives in to the demand for double numbers. He does not give in to the demand for one vote for each member.

The Estates General finally meet on 5 May 1789. Over a thousand deputies meet in the largest hall in the palace at Versailles.

The King and his ministers make very long speeches and everyone has to listen for hours.

The three estates are told to split up and carry on the meeting in three separate halls.

The Third Estate is very angry. Its members fear that the clergy and nobility will simply outvote them, two to one.

The Third Estate demands that the nobles and clergy join them in one, big National Assembly.

They all argue about it for weeks. The Third Estate tells the king that either the nobles and clergy must join them or they will start the work of the Estates General on their own.

Louis is furious.

Background information

What was this unfair voting system all about? You can remind yourself by looking at page 23. Where do you need to say something about this in your narrative?

How can you explain it simply for your reader, in just one or two sentences?

Remember, you don't want to interrupt your story too much, or you will make it dull!

Things happening elsewhere, at the same time

You must decide **where** and **how** you are going to weave in some other developments. Look at these two facts. Where will they fit into the section of the story that you have just written?

> From January 1789, all over France, the people electing the Third Estate are drawing up their *cahiers de doleance*, ready for the meeting of the Estates General.

> In January 1789, the Abbé Sieyès wrote a pamphlet called, 'What is the Third Estate?'. In it, he said that the Third Estate was 'everything'.

You could use words like *Meanwhile... At the same time...* to help you show that they were occurring at the same time. Think about other ways of introducing these facts into your narrative. What do you want the reader to think about their importance?

Why not look in the last chapter to choose a small bit of information about the *cahiers* so that your reader understands

why the third estate wanted to be listened to? Why not look at page 24, to remind yourself what the Abbé Sieyès was writing about? Your reader needs to know that the important members of the Third Estate, the bourgeoisie, were drawing up demands for all kinds of freedoms. They wanted equality with the other two estates. But where is the best place to tell the reader this? You decide.

Smaller details

You now need some smaller details to make this part of your narrative catch your reader's imagination. These details will help your reader to understand what it felt like to be a deputy from the Third Estate at the Estates General.

Here are your details:

> For the very first meeting of the Estates General, the Third Estate are told to wear traditional black clothes.

> The Third Estate has to wait for hours before its members are allowed in.

> The Third Estate is not allowed to enter through the same door as the nobility and clergy.

> The King orders the hall to be prepared by carpenters and painters. Extra pillars and seats are made and velvet and tassels added to them.

> The Third Estate have to sit on plain wooden benches.

Decide where these extra detail might fit. How will you use them? Into which paragraph will you put them? Will you use all of them? (You don't have to!)

Share your ideas with a partner on **where** you are going to build them into your narrative. Share ideas on **how** you are going to build them in. Words like *While... Before... When...* could help you.

In this section you want your reader to feel the mounting anger, the growing frustration and fury of the third estate. How could you sum up these details and make a comment on them? These sentence starters might help:

- *The Third Estate must have been...*

- *The Third Estate would have ...*

- *When the Third Estate were finally allowed in, it was through a special side door. This must have...*

The first meeting of the Estates General. You can see Louis XVI sitting on a throne. The clergy are on his right. The nobles are on his left. The third estate is facing him.

Remember, as the narrator, you *are* allowed to comment!

Now read this section of narrative through very carefully. How does it sound? Can you improve it?

Think

- Look carefully at the picture of the Estates General below. Why do you think the Third Estate were seated so far away from the King?

- What other ideas does this picture give you that you could use in your narrative?

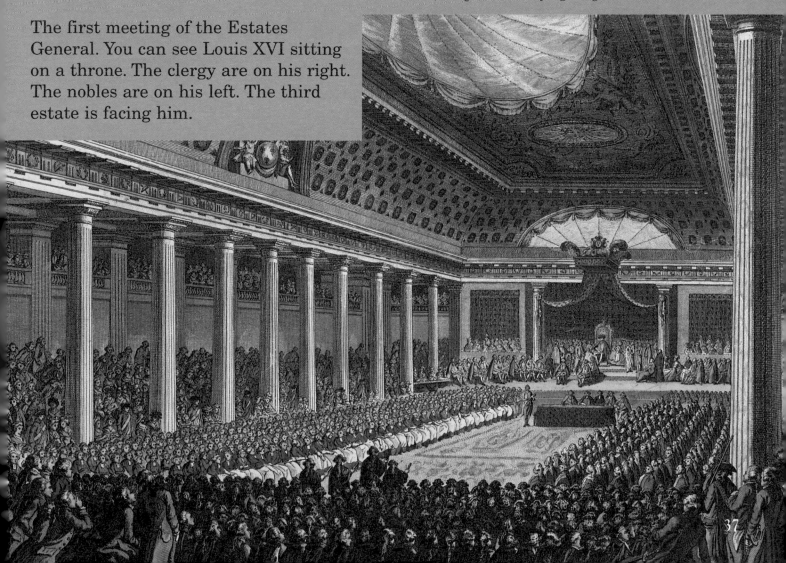

Opening of the Estates General at Versailles, 5 May 1789 by Jan Bulthuis, an eighteenth-century engraving

Part Four: The National Assembly defies the King

Main facts to shape your narrative

Use all the ideas in Steps 1, 2 and 3 to link up these events and make them into an interesting historical narrative.

You will need to decide whether you want to use the very precise dates that you will find below. You might just want to use time connectives such as *When... Then, afterwards... The next day... Soon... Later... Eventually...* or you might want to use the dates. You could use both! Experiment and see which method makes your narrative flow better.

Whatever you do, you cannot just state these events. At the moment you have a boring list of facts. Work out how one flows into the other and why. Try joining some facts up into one sentence and experiment with different ways of doing so. For example

'Desperate to escape from the rain, they poured into a tennis court.'

or

'Pouring into a nearby tennis court, they were glad to escape the pouring rain.'

This bit of the story takes us right up to the Tennis Court Oath, so it is countdown time... Keep up your reader's interest!

Louis decides to hold a special **Royal Session**. He plans to warn the Third Estate not to defy him any more.

19 June, 1789: A few clergy decide to join the Third Estate. Louis is losing control.

20 June: The Third Estate arrives at the palace to find the doors locked and guarded by soldiers. It is raining.

The Third Estate starts to talk angrily about why this has happened. Is Louis trying to break up our meeting by force?

The rain gets worse.

Nearly six hundred Third Estate deputies try to find shelter in the pouring rain.

The deputies find an empty indoor tennis court.

They swear a solemn oath to carry on meeting until they have changed the way France is governed.

23 June: Louis holds his special Royal Session. All three estates go to hear the King. The King orders them to meet separately.

The Third Estate refuses to move.

24 June: 151 clergy join the Third Estate.

25 June: 47 nobles join the Third Estate.

27 June: Louis completely gives in. He orders the nobles and clergy to join the third estate in one, big assembly. This assembly is called the National Assembly. Louis knows that he will have to listen to it.

Before moving on, check that you have linked things up well. As well as facts, you need to use your imagination in an historical narrative, especially when the tension mounts. For example:

- What happened *in between* the finding of the tennis court and the swearing of the oath, do you think?

- What sort of mood do you think the deputies were in?

Look at the painting on page 37 to give you ideas. Remember how cross the deputies were at being locked out. Think about how excited they must have been by the oath. Don't just plonk the facts next to each other. Your job is to **weave** them.

Things happening at the same time elsewhere

Events in Paris at the same time were very important. You need to alert your reader to this. How will you weave this information in without spoiling the flow of your narrative? Think about phrases like, *Meanwhile, in Paris,...* or *While all these events were taking place at Versailles, the people of Paris...*

Here are your things to weave in:

By the end of June, even the Guards, who are supposed to be loyal to the King, are starting to parade the streets of Paris. They are shouting, "Long Live the Third Estate!" and "We are the soldiers of the nation!".

Every night crowds of thousands are gathering in the streets and markets of Paris. They hear the news from Versailles, daily, in journals and pamphlets. Leaders of the crowds are starting to emerge.

During June, the King brings more and more troops into Paris.

Smaller details

In this section you want your reader to **feel the suspense** of these last days. We will give you four separate details which could be very useful to you! As usual, decide **where** they fit into what you have already written. Then decide **how** you will weave them in.

The real reason why the Third Estate deputies cannot not get into the palace on 20 June is that workmen are preparing it for the King's Royal Session. The deputies do not know this.

On 20 June, a leader of the Third Estate called Mirabeau, says, "Nothing can prevent the assembly from continuing its discussions. All members of the assembly shall here and now swear a solemn oath to go on meeting wherever it has to until a constitution for France is set up."

On 23 June, when the Third Estate refuses to move, one of their leaders says to the king, "We shall only leave at the point of bayonets."

On 27 June, crowds in Paris let off fireworks.

As you read through the last part of your historical narrative, think about your last paragraph and your last sentence. Are they powerful and punchy enough? Is the importance of these last events really clear to the reader?

All members of the assembly shall here and now swear a solemn oath to go on meeting wherever it has to until a constitution for France is set up!

Thinking your enquiry through

You have now written a first draft of your historical narrative. But how good is it? Will your reader keep on reading because they want to find out what happened next?

And is it good history? Have you been accurate? Have you selected and positioned your details really well? Does it make the reader think?

There is only one way to find out...

You are now going to take part in a whole-class editorial exercise to make sure that both your narrative and all the others in your class are as good as they can be.

1 Re-read your own narrative. Check each section against the guidance in each Step. Make any improvements. Read some of your paragraphs aloud. How do they sound? Have you got the best possible mixture of short and long sentences?

2 Now swap your narrative with a partner. Using a red pen OR using the 'Comment' function in your wordprocessing tools, make helpful comments on your partner's narrative. Make sure that you read a whole paragraph at a time before commenting. Praise your partner's narrative wherever it is easy to understand and interesting to read.

Now return each narrative to its owner. Read the comments on your own work. Make any necessary changes.

3 Give your narrative to someone not in your year at school – a parent, guardian or grandparent? a brother or sister? a friend from another school? This person will be your 'critical friend'. Ask them to read with two questions in mind:

a) Does your critical friend understand the story? If not, where and why are they confused?

b) Give your critical friend a test: having read your story, are they able to tell you why the Tennis Court Oath happened?

Now make any final changes. Your historical narrative is complete.

Cannon, muskets, fire and smoke

Why have such different stories been told about the storming of the Bastille?

On 14 July 1789, eight thousand people poured through the streets of Paris towards a massive fortress on the edge of the city. The fortress was used as a prison. French people called it the Bastille.

Seventy years later, in 1859, the English writer, Charles Dickens, used the events of that day in a novel called *A Tale of Two Cities*. These extracts are taken from Dickens' story of what happened.

In these extracts, Dickens was giving his own version of one of the most famous events in the history of France – the storming of the Bastille.

Think

- According to these extracts, what was the crowd planning to do when it reached the Bastille?

- What hints does Dickens give about why they were trying to do this?

'Come, then!' cried Defarge, in a resounding voice. 'Patriots and friends, we are ready! The Bastille!'

With a roar that sounded as if all the breath in France had been shaped into the detested word, the living sea rose, wave on wave, depth on depth, and overflowed the city to that point. Alarm-bells ringing, drums beating, the sea raging and thundering on its new beach, the attack begun.

'To me, women!' cried madame his wife. 'What! We can kill as well as the men when the place is taken!' And to her, with a shrill thirsty cry, trooping women variously armed, but all armed alike in hunger and revenge.

Madame Defarge, still heading some of her women, was visible in the inner distance, and her knife was in her hand. Everywhere was tumult, deafening, ...astounding noise...

'The Prisoners!'

'The Records!'

'The secret cells!'

'The instruments of torture!'

'The Prisoners!'

Of all these cries, 'The Prisoners!' was the cry most taken up by the sea that rushed in, as if there were an eternity of people, as well as of time and space.

Extracts from Charles Dickens, A Tale of Two Cities, 1859

A story about past events is not just a description of what happened. Story-telling can be a way of sharing an important belief or giving an opinion about what is right or good. People keep stories from history alive for all kinds of reasons:

This event was a tragedy experienced by all our people. Our shared suffering made us into one people!

This event was a great achievement by our ancestors. We should remain proud of this triumph!

These events changed things forever. If we do not know about them we cannot understand many of our institutions and ideas today.

The things these people did were brave and good. We must celebrate them for ever. Our children must be influenced by these brave, good acts.

This was a terrible wrong and injustice. Future generations must make sure it never happens again.

These people in the past made a huge sacrifice. We benefit from that sacrifice so we should remember and respect what they did for ever!

I haven't really thought why ... why we go on remembering this, but it is **very important** that we do!

The Holocaust

Henry VIII

King John

Armada

1914-1918

Agincourt

Slave Trade

Black Death

1066

Battle of Britain

Oliver Cromwell

(Later, you can decide for yourself which of these reasons explains why people choose to remember the storming of the Bastille today, or whether we need to find another reason altogether...)

Sometimes people tell the same basic story but they tell it in different ways or for different purposes. Sometimes, they re-tell an old story in a fresh way because they want to draw others' attention to something new in it. Sometimes they give it a different slant, emphasise different things or even use their imaginations to make up part of it.

Charles Dickens' novel, *A Tale of Two Cities* is fiction. It is an imaginary love story. It is not the work of an historian. But it is set in an historical period and place – Paris and London during the time of the French Revolution. Dickens describes factual events and details from that time.

As we read Dickens' novel, we discover his views about the French Revolution. His story is more than just an exciting and romantic plot. It also his way of giving an opinion.

Dickens had strong beliefs and views about the French Revolution. He thought that the French Revolution was a wild uprising of the most desperate, poorest people. He believed that they had been driven to madness by hunger and cruelty.

But although Dickens felt that the poor had been wronged, he was horrified by their violence. For Dickens, the violence of the mob was destructive and evil. Above all, he saw revenge as very damaging. He believed that it was a spirit of revenge which later drove the revolutionaries to great cruelty.

When Dickens describes the storming of the Bastille, all these views show through.

Charles Dickens' novel reflects what a lot of 19th century people, both in France and Britain, thought about the events of the French Revolution. It also shaped the way people in Britain thought about the French Revolution for over a hundred years. Many of the images in our heads of the storming of the Bastille come from Dickens' novel. It is a memorable and powerful passage.

But as far as factual history is concerned, quite a lot of it is **wrong**.

- The crowd did **not** storm the Bastille out of revenge.

  - The crowd did **not** storm it to release prisoners. They had other, much more practical reasons for storming it.

  - The people who stormed it were the **not**, in the main, the poorest people in Paris.

In the two hundred years since the French Revolution, the story of the storming of the Bastille has been told in many different ways. As well as different *views*, there are also different *methods* and *purposes* for telling the story:

- There are works of history where historians try to work out what actually happened and why. Historians also try to judge what results it had.

- There are novels and films, paintings and poems, many of which are based very closely on the events. In many of these the artist will have a message or a view about the meaning or importance of the event.

- The story also continues to be told, every year, on the anniversary of the storming of the Bastille, July 14. All over France, traditional celebrations and festivals celebrate the event. This, too, is a kind of story-telling.

Your enquiry

In this enquiry, you will compare three kinds of story about the storming of the Bastille. In each story, you will also detect a different interpretation. Each presents a slightly different view, making its own meaning out of the event.

First, you are going to study Dickens' account of the storming of the Bastille much more closely. You will discover how that novel came about, just how well Dickens told his story, what he was trying to say and why. **Then** you are going to look at what really happened in the storming of the Bastille, by looking at the conclusions of some modern historians who have researched the event. **Finally,** you will look at how and why many French people try to keep the memory of the Bastille alive today.

In order to capture your thinking about the main characteristics of each of these stories, you are going to make three different 'word-pictures' of the storming of the Bastille. At the end of the enquiry you will use your word-pictures to plan a website. This website will explain to other school pupils:

- why these three ways of telling the story are different;

- why each matters and is worth learning about.

A matter of revenge

In the 1850s Charles Dickens saw a play by his friend, the famous author, Wilkie Collins. He was deeply moved by it. The play was called *The Frozen Deep*. In that play, one of two young men sacrifices himself so that the other may enjoy happiness with the girl whom both of them love. Dickens began to plan his own story in which one man sacrifices his life for the other.

But whereas the setting for Wilkie Collins' play was a Polar expedition in the dangerous and unpredictable Arctic, Dickens decided to use another dangerous and unpredictable setting – the French Revolution.

The first edition was published in November 1859. Dickens wrote a letter to Wilkie Collins after he completed the last few pages:

"It has greatly moved and excited me in the doing, and Heaven knows I have done my best and believed in it".

As you read the longer extracts on these pages you can see just what a powerful novel it was and why it has remained so popular. You will also start to picture the Bastille and the crowd. Sometimes historical novels help us to feel a place or an atmosphere better than history books.

Living sea

In this first part, Dickens writes about the crowd surging towards the Bastille. Two of the novel's unpleasant characters appear in this part of the story – Monsieur and Madame Defarge. Monsieur Defarge was master of a wine shop. Madame Defarge was always mysteriously knitting. Later in the novel, we discover that she has been secretly working lots of names into her knitting, in a code. These are the names of those that will be guillotined.

The Defarges are fictional characters. Dickens used them to show us something of the mood of the crowd (as *he* saw it).

Think

- Collect all the words and phrases that suggest deafening noise.

- Pick out all the words and phrases that describe the crowd as rushing water or the sea. What do you think Dickens is trying to say about the crowd through his image of the sea?

- Pick out all the signs that Dickens views the crowd as bloody-thirsty, dangerous or violent.

Keep near to me, Jacques Three,' cried Defarge; 'and you, Jacques One and Two, put yourselves at the head of as many of these patriots as you can. Where is my wife?'

'Eh well! Here you see me!' said madame, composed as ever, but not knitting today. Madame's right hand was occupied with an axe, ... and in her girdle were a pistol and a cruel knife.

'Where do you go, my wife?'

'I go,' said madame, 'with you at present. You shall see me at the head of the women, by-and-by.'

'Come, then!' cried Defarge, in a resounding voice. 'Patriots and friends, we are ready! The Bastille!'

With a roar that sounded as if all the breath in France had been shaped into the detested word, the living sea rose, wave on wave, depth on depth, and overflowed the city to that point. Alarm-bells ringing, drums beating, the sea raging and thundering on its new beach, the attack begun. Deep ditches, double drawbridge, massive stone walls, eight great towers, cannon, muskets, fire and smoke. Through the fire and through the smoke – in the fire and in the smoke, for the sea cast him up against a cannon, and on the instant he became a connonier – Defarge of the wine-shop worked like a manful soldier, Two fierce hours.

Deep ditch, single drawbridge, massive stone walls, eight great towers, cannon, muskets, fire and smoke. One drawbridge down! 'Work, comrades all, work! Work, Jacques One, Jacques Two, Jacques One Thousand, Jacques Two Thousand, Jacques Five-and-Twenty-Thousand; in the name of all the Angels or the Devils – which you prefer – work!' Thus Defarge of the wine-shop, still at his gun, which had long grown hot.

'To me, women!' cried madame his wife. 'What! We can kill as well as the men when the place is taken!' And to her, with a shrill thirsty cry, trooping women variously armed, but all armed alike in hunger and revenge.

Extracts from Charles Dickens, A Tale of Two Cities, 1859

Many films have been made of *A Tale of Two Cities*. **When it comes to the storming of the Bastille, some of them follow the spirit of the Dickens' account very closely. Here are two images from a film made in 1935.**

Images from a British film, A Tale of Two Cities, *made in 1935 by Jack Conway*

Think

- Which ideas and details in the Dickens extract does it look as though the film director used in these two scenes? You should find lots!

Raging sea

Now the battle deepens. As you read (or as you listen to this passage being read to you) try to visualise the scene and hear the noise in your mind. Dickens helps us to imagine the scene with our eyes and our ears.

Cannon, muskets, fire and smoke; but, still the deep ditch, the single drawbridge, the massive stone walls, and the eight great towers. Slight displacements of the raging sea, made by the falling wounded. Flashing weapons, blazing torches, smoking waggon-loads of wet straw, hard work at neighbouring barricades in all directions, shrieks, volleys, execrations, bravery without stint, boom, smash and rattle and the furious sounding of the living sea; but, still the deep ditch, and the single drawbridge, and the massive stone walls, and the eight great towers, and still Defarge of the wine-shop at his gun, grown doubly hot by the service of Four fierce hours.

A white flag from within the fortress, and a parley – this dimly perceptible through the raging storm, nothing audible in it – suddenly the sea rose immeasurably wider and higher, and swept Defarge of the wine-shop over the lowered drawbridge, past the massive stone outer walls, in among the eight great towers surrendered!

So resistless was the force of the ocean bearing him on, that even to draw his breath or turn his head was as impracticable as if he had been struggling in the surf at the South Sea, until he was landed in the outer court-yard of the Bastille. There, against an angle of a wall, he made a struggle to look about him. Jacques Three was nearly at his side; Madame Defarge, still heading some of her women, was visible in the inner distance, and her knife was in her hand. Everywhere was tumult, exultation, deafening and maniacal bewilderment, astounding noise...

'The Prisoners!'
'The Records!'
'The secret cells!'
'The instruments of torture!'
'The Prisoners!'

Of all these cries, 'The Prisoners!' was the cry most taken up by the sea that rushed in, as if there were an eternity of people, as well as of time and space.

Charles Dickens, A Tale of Two Cities, 1859

Think

● What do we learn from this extract about how difficult it was to attack the Bastille?

● Collect some more words and phrases that help us to hear the loud noise.

● Collect more words and phrases that describe the crowd as flowing water.

● With which words does Dickens create a feeling that the crowd was now an unstoppable force, taking on a life of its own?

Remorseless sea

In this passage, Dickens describes what happens to the governor of the Bastille. The governor is not a fictional character. He was called De Launay. Several sources from this period seem to confirm that he was dragged along by the crowd, murdered and had his head hacked off with a knife. Dickens describes him as a 'grim old officer' wearing grey and red. He uses this bloody incident to show the lack of pity in the crowd.

In the howling universe of passion... that seemed to encompass this grim old officer in his grey coat and red decoration, there was but one quite steady figure, and that was a woman's. She stood immovable close to the grim old officer, and remained immovable close to him; remained immovable close to him though the streets, as Defarge and the rest bore him along; remained immovable close to him when he was got near his destination, and began to strike at him from behind; remained immovable close to him when the long-gathering rain of stabs and blows fell heavy; was so close to him when he dropped dead under it, that, she put her foot upon his neck, and with her cruel knife – long ready – hewed off his head.

The hour was come when Saint Antoine* was to execute its horrible idea of hoisting up men for lamps to show what he could be and do. Saint Antoine's blood was up, and the blood of tyranny and domination by the iron hand was down – down on the steps of the Hotel de Ville where the governor's body lay – down on the sole of the shoe of Madame Defarge where she had trodden on the body to steady it for mutilation.

The sea of black and threatening waters, and of destructive upheaving of wave against wave, whose depths were yet unfathomed and whose forces were yet unknown. The remorseless sea of sway shapes, voices of vengeance, and faces hardened in the furnaces of suffering until the touch of pity could make no mark on them.

Charles Dickens, A Tale of Two Cities, 1859

*Saint Antoine was the district of Paris close to the Bastille where many workers lived.

Look again at the sentence in red. This was Dickens' way of saying that the people of Saint Antoine would soon cut off heads of those they had killed and hang them up from lamp posts for people to see. This was what the crowd did to the governor of the Bastille. Dickens was also hinting at more gruesome developments to come – the use of the guillotine.

Think

- Which parts of this extract suggest a spirit of revenge and bitterness?

- How does Dickens suggest that there may be worse violence and destruction to come?

- What do you think Dickens was saying *about the crowd* in his last paragraph? Look carefully at the underlined words and phrases.

Here is another shot from the 1935 film. It is a close-up of the crowd. Look at their faces and clothes. Notice what they are carrying. The film director has used all kinds of ideas in the Dickens extracts that you have just read.

Images from a British film, A Tale of Two Cities, made in 1935 by Jack Conway

STEP 1

Draw your own simple outline picture of the Bastille. An outline of strong walls and eight strong towers will be enough. Turn it into a 'word-picture' that represents *Dickens'* story of the storming of the Bastille. Put key words and phrases all over your picture such as *revenge*, *hunger*, *boom*, *smash* and *rattle*. You could also be creative with the water images that Dickens uses, arranging your words in swirls and torrents to show Dickens' idea of the crowd as an unstoppable sea.

Understanding Charles Dickens' version of the story

Ideas and experiences

When he chose to write so vividly about the storming of the Bastille, Dickens was influenced by his own experiences. These experiences shaped some of the ideas that showed through in his novel.

When Dickens was a small boy, his father spent time in prison for being in debt. With no money for an education Dickens had to work in a factory. He was distressed, powerless and fearful that his father would never get out of prison.

A Tale of Two Cities is full of the theme of prisons and imprisonment. A key character in the novel was imprisoned for 27 years in the Bastille.

So much imprisonment is unjust, wrong and creates yet more problems than it solves!

Dickens tasted real poverty as a child. It was a shock. He also continued to observe poverty and suffering all around him, especially in Britain's towns and cities.

There is no escape for the poor from injustice and terrible conditions. If there is no escape, they will turn to desperate measures!

Many of Dickens' novels include comments on suffering of the poor. He writes about social injustice. *A Tale of Two Cities* is no exception.

We must not allow men to become mobs! If the world is violently overturned we will always live in a state of violence.

Dickens was horrified by the destructive violence that could result when a mob of people acted together in rage, hatred or revenge. He believed that violence would only lead to more violence and no good could come from it.

In *A Tale of Two Cities*, Dickens captures some of the worst violence and bloodshed carried out by the revolutionaries. In his account of the storming of the Bastille, Dickens is hinting ahead at future behaviour of the crowd which he considered evil.

Places and people

Visits to France and meetings with historians were also important in shaping Dickens' story:

Dickens visited Paris several times during the fifteen years before he wrote his novel.

> I know the streets of Paris well – I can write about it as well as I can write about London.

In *A Tale of Two Cities* Dickens has many accurate and detailed descriptions of streets and buildings in Paris.

On one of his many visits to Paris, Dickens met the historian Michelet. Michelet was one of the first historians to write about the French Revolution. Michelet said that the whole revolution was a spontaneous outburst. It was an uprising of the whole French nation against tyranny, poverty and injustice.

> The common people – the peasants and the city poor – have rebelled against the cruelty and injustice of kings and aristocrats. They are the real heroes of the revolution!

> Michelet's view about the causes of the revolution, I will use. But I **cannot** show the crowd as **heroes!** Their violence led to worse violence. I will show that poverty and suffering turned the crowd into **violent madmen**.

In the early chapters of *A Tale of Two Cities*, Dickens paints a picture of both hope and hatred arising and spreading spontaneously in all French people. He makes his story of the storming of the Bastille into an outburst of popular feeling.

Like historians of his time, Dickens saw the French Revolution as an angry outburst of a whole people against poverty and cruelty. As you know from Enquiries 1 and 2, this is far too simple as an explanation of the French Revolution! But until the mid-twentieth century, it was a very common explanation.

Sometimes when one person or group of people tells a story powerfully, that meaning catches on for everyone. This is one reason why Charles Dickens' novel is so important. His novel influenced popular views of the French Revolution for some time.

Language and facts

There is yet another reason why Dickens chose revolutionary France as his setting for his story. In 1840 he met an historian called Thomas Carlyle. In *The French Revolution* (1839), Carlyle wrote in a strange and powerful way. He described the storming of the Bastille dramatically, full of symbols and spiritual meaning. Dickens fell completely under Carlyle's spell. He was fascinated by the weird and wonderful Carlyle and fascinated by his book.

We can only give you a taste of Carlyle's extraordinary writings here. But you only need to read a little to see just how important Carlyle was in shaping Dickens' account of the storming of the Bastille. Dickens borrowed from Carlyle not only *ideas* and *facts*, but also some of his *language*.

Think

As you read the tiny extracts by Carlyle, collect examples of each of the following **five** things:

- images of **water**;

- descriptions of loud **noise**;

- all kinds of **factual details** that Dickens' clearly borrowed for use in the extract you read above;

- the crowd getting **out of control**, taking on a dangerous life of its own;

- **ideas about violence** which seem to be similar to those of Dickens.

Here are some examples of Carlyle's writing:

Paris is in the streets; rushing, foaming like some Venice wine-glass into which you had dropped poison.

And so it roars, and rages, and brays; drums beating, steeples pealing;

criers rushing with hand-bells.

How the multitude flows on, welling through every street: the Suburb Saint-Antoine rolling hitherward wholly, as one man!

On, then, all Frenchmen that have hearts in their bodies! Roar with all your throats, of cartilage and metal, ye Sons of Liberty; stir whatsoever is in you, soul, body or spirit; for it is the hour! Smite, ...smite at that outer drawbridge chain, though the fiery hail whistles round thee! Never did thy axe strike such a stroke. Down with it, man; down with it ... let the whole accursed **Edifice** sink..., and tyranny be swallowed up for ever! ... the chain yields, breaks; the huge drawbridge slams down, thundering. Glorious: and yet, alas, it is still but the outworks. Eight grim towers still soar aloft intact. Ditch yawning impassable; ...the inner drawbridge with its back towards us: the Bastille is still to take!

...the roar of the multitude grows deep. Paris has got to the height of its frenzy; whirled, all ways, by panic madness. At every street-barricade, there whirls simmering, a minor whirlpool.

Here are some more extracts from Carlyle's writing:

O poor mortals, how ye make this Earth bitter for each other; this fearful and wonderful life fearful and horrible; and Satan has his place in all hearts!

Noise as of the Crack of Doom!

Straw is burnt; three cartloads of it go up in white smoke: almost choking **patriotism** itself;

It was a living deluge, plunging headlong.

De Launay, 'discovered in gray frock with poppy-coloured riband,' ... Miserable de Launay! ...The bleeding trunk lies on the steps there; the head is off through the streets; ghastly, aloft on a pike.

Brothers, your wrath is cruel! full of fierce bellowings, and thirst of blood. One other officer is massacred; one other is hanged on the lamp-iron:

Vengeance: blaze of triumph on a dark ground of terror: all outward, all inward things fallen into one general wreck of madness!

O Friends, stain not with blood the greenest laurels ever gained in this world!

Carlyle used sources from the time, especially military ones, for some of the details. His use of detail and colour helps us to imagine the scene vividly.

At the same time, Carlyle treated the Bastille as a **metaphor** for the *ancien regime*. Like many writers at this time, he saw the old feudal society as a house or a building. He was saying that it was really beliefs and ideas, not physical force, that create or destroy things.

For Carlyle, the destruction of the Bastille was a symbol of the destruction of old feudal France by the *philosophes* – the writers whose ideas you found out about in Enquiry 1. The storming of the Bastille by *force* was therefore a symbol of a kind of 'storming' of the old France by *ideas*.

STEP 2

Now you know a lot more about why Dickens wrote about the storming of the Bastille in the way that he did. You can now expand your word picture.

Underneath and around the word picture you made for Step One, add words and phrases which show where Dickens' view of the storming of the Bastille came from. Use his experiences and encounters with historians and their writings. You could experiment with some short sentences capturing Dickens' beliefs and views, such as, 'violence leads to violence'. You could also include examples of Carlyle's language.

A military matter

The account by Dickens is very important. It was a fine piece of writing and it helps to explain many nineteenth-century views about the storming of the Bastille. But what really happened?

Of course, Dickens was not *entirely* wrong about revenge. The crowd surging towards the Bastille would have been full of local stories about dungeons and torture chambers. But there was actually a much more practical and down-to-earth reason for attacking the Bastille...

It is time for another kind of story – the kind that is told by modern historians. We will begin where we left off in Enquiry 2, with the Third Estate and the new National Assembly.

The King gathers troops around Paris

On 27 June 1789, it looked as though the King had finally given in. He ordered the nobles and clergy to join the Third Estate in one big assembly. It looked as though the King would have to listen to this National Assembly.

But had the King *really* given in?

Had the King *really* accepted defeat?

Was the King *really* trying to buy time, so that he could gather troops to crush the Assembly?

We do not know the answers to these questions. What matters is that people *at the time* were asking them. In early July, lots of people were very jumpy:

- The deputies of the Third Estate at Versailles were jumpy. After all that had happened, they did not trust the King.

  Supposing the King tries to dissolve our assembly and arrest our leaders?

- The workers on the streets of Paris were jumpy. They were still angry at the high price of bread and unemployment.

  Why is the King gathering more and more troops around Paris?

- The journalists and politicians were jumpy. Night after night, revolutionary speakers like Camille Desmoulins made fiery speeches. Thousands gathered to listen to them.

We must deliver the King from his evil advisers!

Whatever the King was up to, there is no doubt that the number of troops in Paris had been growing since early June. Many of these troops were foreign. There were German cavalry troops right in the centre of Paris. This made the Parisians even angrier. The King said that they were there to keep order.

But on 26 June he suddenly summoned another **4800** soldiers.

On 1 July, he summoned another **11,500**.

By 11 July there were just under **30,000 soldiers in Paris**.

Rumours easily spread:

The King is planning to disperse the National Assembly by force!

The search for arms

It only needed a trigger for Paris to revolt. That trigger came on 12 July when news reached Paris that the King had dismissed his finance minister, Necker. Unlike the King's other advisers, Necker was popular with the people of Paris. They had faith in him as someone who could help. But now he was dismissed.

This convinced the crowds that King was going to use troops to regain control. If the King felt strong enough to dismiss a popular minister, what could stop him now? With so many troops he could take on the National Assembly and arrest its leaders! With so many troops he might try to silence the crowds and their leaders in Paris! It was time to act.

The Parisian crowds quickly became active. The revolutionary speakers called on the crowds to take up arms. The crowd began a two-day search for weapons. They raided gun shops and swordsmiths. They searched for muskets and ammunition.

Many of the King's troops stood by and took no action against the crowds. Some royal troops even started to listen to the revolutionary speakers at the Palais Royal. Order started to break down. Many of the poorest Parisians decided to attack the hated customs posts around the city. These customs posts were ten-feet high barriers where special taxes on food had to be paid, making food prices even higher. Angry crowds tore down 40 of them.

Worried by the disorder, the Paris electors (who had chosen the deputies in the Estates General) decided to form a National Guard. This was a special army of citizens designed to keep order and to defend the city against the King's troops.

So the people now had their own troops. But they still needed more arms...

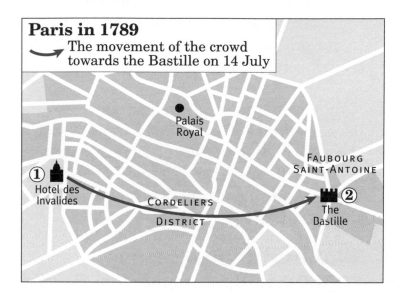

Paris in 1789
The movement of the crowd towards the Bastille on 14 July

If you look on the map of Paris you can see what happened next. About 8000 people headed for the Hotel des Invalides (find 1 on the map). This was a retirement home for old soldiers but it was also a weapon store. There the crowd seized over 28,000 muskets and 20 cannon.

But they were still short of gunpowder and cartridges. Rumours spread that there were tonnes of gunpowder in the Bastille (2 on the map). The crowd, together with some of the National Guard, made for the Bastille.

Find the Bastille on the map. It is close to the Faubourg Saint-Antoine. Here many workers lived, both skilled furniture makers and poorer workers. These people had spent their lives staring up at this fortress, a symbol of the King's power.

The fall of the Bastille: reasons and results

There were no **plans** to storm the Bastille at all. Two representatives went in to persuade the governor to hand over ammunition. Meanwhile, the crowd grew impatient. A few broke into the inner courtyard. The governor ordered his troops to fire on them. Some members of the crowd were killed.

A full-scale attack on the fortress then developed. The King's troops did not stop the attack. About 5 out of 6 battalions deserted. Some actually joined in with the Parisians in the attack. They simply changed sides!

The main short-term reason

for the storming of the Bastille was to get arms and ammunition to protect the people of Paris against the King's troops. They were not trying to release prisoners (they did find some prisoners inside, but only seven!).

The main short-term result

of the storming of the Bastille was the removal of the King's military power. Instead, the people of Paris now had arms. The King had no troops to support him.

Many of the King's troops, the French Guards, had sympathy with the people. Perhaps some were influenced by the revolutionary speakers. Perhaps the rest just knew the King's number was up.

This picture was painted only a few years later. It shows the captured governor, De Launay.

Think

- Look carefully at the painting and list the different kinds of people that you think you can see.

The Storming of the Bastille and the Arrest of Joseph Delaunay, a painting by Charles Thevenin, 1789-1793

Read what some modern historians have written:

R. R. Palmer, writing in 1971, summed it up like this:

Professor T.C.W. Blanning reached this conclusion when he was writing a book about the French Revolution in 1998:

Paris became very restless at the news that troops were concentrating about the city. Actually, the troops had no definite orders. No one knew what to do, and Louis XVI was not the sort of man to shoot down his own subjects. From July 12 (1789) there were clashes between parties of soldiers and gatherings of civilians. Groups under unplanned leadership began to search for arms... Word spread that arms were stored at the Bastille ... the crowd that swarmed about the Bastille on the 14 July was not concerned with the prisoners but in general was protesting against dark and unknown forces threatening the people and in particular was asking for weapons.

R.R. Palmer (1971) The World of the French Revolution,

When the revolutionary crowd attacked the Bastille, they were not seeking to liberate political prisoners or to destroy a symbol of the old regime, they were looking for arms and ammunition with which to equip their new military force, the National Guard. That is the true importance of 14 July 1789 – it marked the collapse of the regime's most valuable asset: its control of disciplined armed force. Once that had been broken, the Revolution had come to stay.

T.W.C.Blanning (1998), The French Revolution: Class War or Culture Clash,

Think

- The search for arms was the main short-term reason for the storming of the Bastille. If you were explaining why the storming of the Bastille happened, what other causes would you mention? Look back at everything you have read on pages 55 to 56.

'The crowd' in Paris

Today, when we picture the storming of the Bastille, the thing we still visualise is people surging forwards to take control of a fortress. It must have been a remarkable event, thousands of people taking action together. Historians call these people 'the crowd'.

In the second half of the twentieth century, historians started to take a great interest in this crowd. It raises all kinds of fascinating historical questions:

In the nineteenth century (when Charles Dickens was writing his novel) many historians assumed that the Parisian crowd was made up of the very poor, criminals and vagrants. As you have seen, films of *A Tale of Two Cities* show people in rags, down-and-outs hurling themselves into the crowd out of hunger.

Much more recently, historians have used sources from the time to trace the professions of about 700-800 members of the crowd that stormed the Bastille. They have found out the following:

About five sixths were skilled craftsmen (such as joiners, locksmiths, cobblers, clockmakers), shopkeepers and other small tradesmen, clerks and journeymen. There were some labourers and wage-earning workers but nearly all were *skilled* workmen or 'artisans'.

About one sixth was made up of richer tradesmen – including some factory owners and merchants - soldiers, officers and a handful from the professions (such as lawyers, doctors and teachers).

All these people lived within two kilometres of the Bastille.

These were the kinds of people who had listened to the revolutionary speeches outside the Palais Royal. These were the people who had eagerly awaited news of what was happening in Versailles during June. Some of them would have been able to read journals and pamphlets spreading revolutionary ideas.

These people would also have suffered from the very high prices and unemployment. Bread reached its highest price ever on 14 July. They were not the kinds of people who had property or savings. But they were not the starving jobless or homeless either.

Later in the Revolution, in about the spring of 1792, these kinds of people started to be called the ***sans culottes***. This means 'without breeches'. The humbler sort of people – tradesmen and craftsmen – did not wear the knee breeches worn by the bourgeoisie and the aristocracy. Instead they wore long trousers.

The *sans culottes* wore red caps with a *tricolore*, the symbol of the revolution. Men and women addressed one another as *citoyen* and *citoyenne* (citizen). They saw themselves as defenders of the Revolution.

The Singer Chenard as a Sans Culotte, from a painting by Louis Leopold Bouilly, 1792

It was only the more organised groups of workers in Paris who later started to be called *sans culottes*. The main centre for the *sans culottes* was the Cordeliers District of Paris (find it on the map on page 57). In 1790, they founded one of the more radical political clubs, the Cordeliers Club.

The crowd and the *sans culottes* are of great interest to historians because it is unusual to see such large numbers of ordinary people influencing events in this way. We still have a lot more to find out about them. Historians still argue about who they were, exactly, about just how important they were and about why they acted as they did at different stages in the revolution.

What we **do** know is that the crowd that stormed the Bastille contained many of the sorts of the people who later called themselves *sans culottes*. At that stage, in July 1789, they were not yet very organised. Economic distress, radical political ideas and anger at the King's actions came together to send them out on the streets.

This coming out onto the streets turned out to be very significant, for it was the first of many. As you will find out, the crowd continued to be active at key stages in the revolution, organising people and influencing events.

But even in July 1789, they were not just a hungry, angry mob. They were not 'down-and-outs'. Although the Bastille certainly was a hated symbol, they were not attacking the Bastille just out of 'hunger and revenge' as Dickens would have us believe. As you have discovered, they had a very practical reason for attacking it …

… and it had nothing to do with releasing the prisoners.

STEP 3

You are now going to make a second word picture. Draw another simple outline of the Bastille. Choose and arrange words and phrases to present what really happened, its short-term reasons and results.

For example you could include words such as:

- gunpowder,

- cartridges (for the muskets)

- cannon.

What words might you use to describe the sort of people who were in the crowd? What words and phrases might you use to show the military importance of the event?

Outside the walls of the Bastille, you could think of a way of showing how the King's forces switched sides. Choose some words or phrases from the extracts by the modern historians.

A symbol of liberty

The storming of the Bastille created a **myth**. This myth is still celebrated today in the French national festival – Bastille Day – every 14 July. According to this myth, the action of the ordinary people of Paris forced a revolution to happen in the name of **liberty**.

As you now know, the reality was rather different:

> The causes of the French Revolution were **much** more complicated!

> The causes of the storming of the Bastille itself were **much** more basic!

Groups of people and nations often want stories remembered by future generations. They make sure that that story is commemorated, celebrated or preserved. Sometimes they seek to educate others. Sometimes people want a story remembered because they arc proud of it, because it reminds them of important struggles for freedom or justice in the past.

When this happens, it is very common for people to choose those parts of the story that they want to emphasise and to ignore others. The significance of the story for *today* sometimes becomes more important than examining its actual significance *at the time*.

The celebration of Bastille Day is one important way in which modern French people try to keep the story of the French Revolution alive today. The storming of the Bastille is seen as a symbol of the whole French Revolution.

Every year, on 14 July, there is a military parade on the Champs-Elysees in the presence of the French President. On 14 July 2003 nearly 4,000 troops, 350 tanks, jeeps and other vehicles and more than 280 horses took part in the parade, while 76 aircraft flew above.

By finding out what modern French people say, write and do to remember the storming of the Bastille, we learn more about what is important to them. Study the modern website extracts on page 64 carefully. The first is from a French website for children. It has been written to help young tourists from other countries to understand France. The second extract is from the French Embassy's website in the United States.

As you read them, compare them with what you now know, from historians, about what really happened. Think carefully about why each extract was written and what it is trying to achieve. Who is it **for**? What has the author chosen as **important**?

An extract from a French website for tourists called *Holiday Fun*:

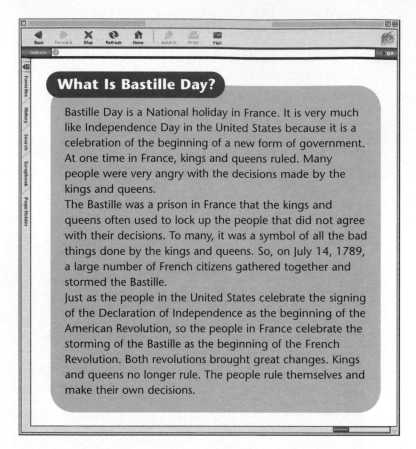

What Is Bastille Day?

Bastille Day is a National holiday in France. It is very much like Independence Day in the United States because it is a celebration of the beginning of a new form of government. At one time in France, kings and queens ruled. Many people were very angry with the decisions made by the kings and queens.

The Bastille was a prison in France that the kings and queens often used to lock up the people that did not agree with their decisions. To many, it was a symbol of all the bad things done by the kings and queens. So, on July 14, 1789, a large number of French citizens gathered together and stormed the Bastille.

Just as the people in the United States celebrate the signing of the Declaration of Independence as the beginning of the American Revolution, so the people in France celebrate the storming of the Bastille as the beginning of the French Revolution. Both revolutions brought great changes. Kings and queens no longer rule. The people rule themselves and make their own decisions.

Think

- You now know a lot about why the Bastille was stormed. What do you think of the explanation given for the storming of the Bastille in the third paragraph?

- Why do you think that the story is told in such a simple way here?

- In what ways is the modern myth about the causes of the storming of the Bastille similar to the views of some of the nineteenth-century historians you read about on page 6o?

An extract from the French Embassy website in the United States:

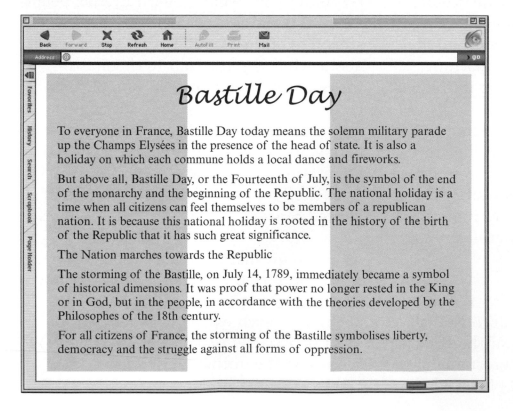

Bastille Day

To everyone in France, Bastille Day today means the solemn military parade up the Champs Elysées in the presence of the head of state. It is also a holiday on which each commune holds a local dance and fireworks.

But above all, Bastille Day, or the Fourteenth of July, is the symbol of the end of the monarchy and the beginning of the Republic. The national holiday is a time when all citizens can feel themselves to be members of a republican nation. It is because this national holiday is rooted in the history of the birth of the Republic that it has such great significance.

The Nation marches towards the Republic

The storming of the Bastille, on July 14, 1789, immediately became a symbol of historical dimensions. It was proof that power no longer rested in the King or in God, but in the people, in accordance with the theories developed by the Philosophes of the 18th century.

For all citizens of France, the storming of the Bastille symbolises liberty, democracy and the struggle against all forms of oppression.

Think

- According to the French Embassy website, why is Bastille Day important **today**?

- Why do you think that this website might have been created? For what kind of reader do you think it might have been designed?

You are now ready to make your third and final word picture of the Bastille.

Using page 63 to 64, fill your Bastille outline with words and phrases that capture the meaning of the storming of the Bastille to French people today. For example, you might choose *celebration*, *parade in Champs Elysees*, *republican nation*, *national holiday*, *democracy*, *a new form of government*. Decide how you are going to arrange these words and phrases so that they link up and explain each other. See what else you can find out about the celebration of Bastille Day today from your own research.

Thinking your enquiry through

You are going to plan a website to help other pupils of your age to understand why there are different ways of telling the story of the storming of the Bastille.*

Each of your word pictures shows how different people have made meaning out of the storming of the Bastille. Often, people tell the same basic story but they tell it in different ways and for different purposes. For some people, keeping the memory alive is more important than working out *exactly* what happened. This is how a story takes on a different significance in another age. We need to understand how and why this happens.

Your challenge is to explain how these differing stories come about. Design three sections, each one will include and explain one of your word pictures:

A matter of revenge

Include a description of Dickens' novel. Choose some quotations to give a flavour of it. Explain how Dickens came to describe the storming of the Bastille in the way that he did. Remember to enthuse your readers about Dickens' wonderful novel. Explain how and why it has been important in influencing views and mental pictures of the storming of the Bastille for generations.

It would be a good idea to look up *A Tale of Two Cities*. See what else you can find that may interest your reader. You may end up reading the whole novel yourself ...

A military matter

Write a summary of what actually happened at the storming of the Bastille and why. Explain why the storming of the Bastille was important at the time. Include some of the material that recent historians' have found out about the crowd. Tell your readers something about the important historical questions concerning the crowd.

A symbol of freedom

Explain why the storming of the Bastille is important today. Using your own research you could use some short extracts from modern websites or from French newspapers. You could include your own picture of Bastille Day celebrations, explaining carefully what is taking place and why.

*You may even be able to create a real website which your teacher can use with next year's pupils.

Royal Blood

What made the revolutionaries kill the King?

This painting of the royal family was made in 1775. It shows Louis XVI walking with his family in the grounds of Versailles. Louis (in the red coat) is walking behind the family and is talking to one of his ministers.

Think

- What message do you think the artist wanted to give about Louis?

On the day the Bastille was attacked Louis XVI had been out all day hunting in the grounds of Versailles. In the evening he was tired, and he wrote only one word in his diary, "Rien" (Nothing). Some historians think this shows just how out of touch the King was, but his journal was really a record of the animals Louis killed (or failed to kill!) in the hunt.

Later that night, around eleven o'clock, the King was woken by one of his **courtiers**. The courtier told Louis the full story of the fall of the Bastille. "Is it a revolt?", asked the King. "No sire, it is a revolution", replied the courtier. Louis listened to the horrific account of de Launay's death. He realised what this meant. His soldiers in Paris had been defeated. He could no longer hope to use force against the **National Assembly**.

The following day, Louis went to the National Assembly. He arrived on foot, accompanied only by his two brothers. In his speech the King denied that he had planned any action against the **National Assembly**. He promised to order the withdrawal of his troops from Paris. This pleased the deputies. They thought that the King had been misled by his nobles, but had finally been brought to his senses. The deputies felt that Louis now deserved their loyalty. In the National Assembly they cheered their King.

Only three and a half years later the deputies voted to execute Louis XVI.

Your enquiry

When the revolution started in 1789 most people thought that the King should continue to be the head of the government. The idea of killing the King would have seemed deeply shocking. But by 1793 the revolutionaries had decided that the King should die. In this enquiry you will find out why things changed between 1789 and 1793. As you read about the events you will make an execution chart to show why the revolutionaries turned against the King.

The weeks after the storming of the Bastille

After the storming of the Bastille disorder spread from Paris throughout France.

In the countryside, during the summer of 1789, peasants attacked chateaux, abbeys and tax offices. The peasants heard wild rumours that the nobles were paying bandits to take revenge. They also heard that foreign armies were preparing to invade. Fear created panic and more violence. The peasants beat up bailiffs and set fire to manorial records. They claimed that they were acting in the name of the King against the wicked nobles.

In towns all over France workers rioted when the price of bread became too high. They attacked the houses of town

officials and several officials were killed. The workers believed that their King wanted them to be properly fed. Like the peasants, the urban workers claimed to be acting in the King's name.

During August the National Assembly made two revolutionary changes:

1. On the evening of 4 August, the noble deputies in the National Assembly stood up, one by one, and announced that they would give up their feudal rights. By the following morning the tithe, the *corvée*, hunting rights and labour services had all been abolished. Feudalism was dead.

2. On 26 October The National Assembly agreed to the Declaration of the Rights of Man and the Citizen. This was a long and important document which set out exactly how the people of France were to be treated equally and fairly.

These changes were supposed to make France a fairer country, but did not mean the end of the monarchy. Everyone in the National Assembly thought that the King should still be the head of government. But Louis XVI refused to give his consent to the end of feudalism or the Declaration of the Rights of Man and the Citizen.

For the ordinary people of Paris life got harder in the weeks after the storming of the Bastille. Unemployment was increasing and bread was in short supply. The 1789 harvest had been good, but a drought in August meant that millers could not use their water mills to grind the corn. In September fighting broke out in the bread queues. Bakers suspected of hoarding grain were attacked, and soldiers had to be posted in the bakeries.

At the end of September, a regiment of the King's soldiers arrived at Versailles from Flanders. The people of Paris suspected that the King might be planning to use force against the National Assembly. On the evening of 1 October, Louis gave a banquet to welcome the Flanders Regiment. This turned out to be disastrous for the King.

At the banquet the King's soldiers wore red, white and blue cockades (badges) in their hats. In the summer of 1789, the revolutionaries had adopted this *tricolore* symbol of red, white and blue. Red and blue were the colours of Paris, while white was the colour of the royal family. Several of the guests got drunk. They insulted the National Assembly and cheered the royal family. Worst of all, some of the soldiers tore off their *tricolore* cockades and replaced them with white ones!

In Paris, the next day, the newspapers claimed that the soldiers had trampled on the *tricolore* cockades. The mood turned very nasty. It was time for action.

The women march to Versailles, October 1789

5 October 1789 was a wet and miserable day in Paris. The women who worked in the markets could no longer afford bread to feed their families. They were hungry and angry. Stories of the 1 October banquet made them even more furious. The market women decided to do something drastic. They would march to the King's palace at Versailles and demand bread from the King himself.

At 10 o'clock, the women set off in the drenching rain for Versailles. More and more women, and some men, joined the march. Not all the women joined in willingly. A nurse called Jeanne Martin was forced to march by a group of about forty women who threatened to beat her up if she did not join them. Soon, about 6,000 women were tramping through the driving rain.

At five o'clock, the market women arrived at Versailles. They were bedraggled and hungry after their long walk in the rain. The King's soldiers stopped them entering the palace grounds, but the women had no difficulty entering the National Assembly, nearby. The muddy, wet women plonked themselves down next to the deputies in their posh clothes. They shouted loudly "We want bread". A few of the women were drunk and vomited over the benches. The deputies were alarmed. They promised to do everything they could to make sure that Paris was supplied with grain. But the women demanded a meeting with the King himself.

Louis was out hunting (where else!). When he heard what was happening, he rode his horse at top speed back to the palace. His ministers urged him to escape. Marie

Think

● What weapons do the women have?

● What message does the artist want to give about the mood of the crowd?

Some of the women marching on Versailles in October 1789, an eighteenth century engraving

Antoinette also tried to persuade her husband to flee. Louis could not make up his mind, but in the end he decided that he did not want to become a King in hiding, and decided to stay. Bravely, he agreed to meet with a small group of the women.

Pierrette Chabry, a seventeen year old flower-seller, was chosen as spokeswoman. She asked the King for bread, and Louis replied, "I will order all the bread in Versailles to be collected and given to you". Pierrette was so nervous that she then fainted. Louis gave her smelling salts and helped her to her feet. Later that afternoon the King agreed to accept both the abolition of feudalism and the Declaration of the Rights of Man. The crisis seemed to have passed. Thinking that the trouble was over, Louis sent his soldiers back to their barracks. In the early hours of the morning he went to bed.

At four o'clock in the morning, the Queen woke suddenly. She heard loud shouts and yells outside her door, "Where is she? Where is the whore? We'll wring her neck!"

A large group of angry men and women had broken into the palace. They had already killed two of the Queen's bodyguards, hacking off their heads with an axe. The Queen and her ladies dashed out of the room, ran up the secret staircase which led to the King's chamber, and locked the doors behind them. Minutes later the mob broke down the Queen's door. Finding the bed empty, they slashed the covers with their swords and pikes.

As daylight broke over Versailles, the crowd had gathered in the courtyard under the King's balcony. They demanded to see the King and Queen. "To Paris!, To Paris!", they shouted. The royal family had no choice. At twelve-thirty, a huge procession set off from Versailles on the seven hour journey to Paris. In the middle Louis, Marie Antoinette and their two children were slumped in the royal carriage. Behind them was a trail of carts filled with flour from the palace bins. The market women joked that they were taking, "The baker, the baker's wife and the baker's boy", back to Paris.

STEP 1

It's time to begin your execution chart. The first part of your chart will cover the events from July to October 1789. Make a chart like the one below.

Execution Chart

July 1789 – January 1793	
Summary of Events	Why the Revolutionaries turned against the King
Use this space to make a summary of events	Use this space to explain why the Revolutionaries turned against the King

Prisoners in Paris, Autumn 1789 to Spring 1791

The royal family were taken to the Tuileries, a run-down palace in the centre of Paris. The **Dauphin** had to spend the first night in a room barricaded with furniture because the door did not shut. "It's very ugly here, mother", he said. In the weeks which followed, life became more normal at the Tuileries. The Assembly allowed the royal family generous living expenses. Marie Antoinette worked at her tapestry with her ladies, and Louis taught her to play billiards. The King was even allowed to hunt.

Nevertheless the King was forced to accept three huge limitations on his power:

1 He was made to surrender his own bodyguards.
2 He had to accept the new constitution agreed by the Assembly

3 He had to accept that he now ruled under the law, and not by divine right.

Unwillingly, Louis was becoming a constitutional monarch.

On 14 July 1790 representatives from all over France were invited to celebrate the anniversary of the fall of the Bastille on the Champ de Mars in Paris. The painting below shows some of the 300,000 people at the celebration.

In the centre of the painting you can see the altar where the leaders of the revolution swore an oath to be faithful to the nation. Louis was not allowed near the altar. He sat at the side and, although he made a speech promising to support the National Assembly's new **constitution**, many people felt that he was only accepting the revolution grudgingly.

Over the next few months, the King and the revolutionaries became bitterly divided. The problem was the church. The Assembly decided that bishops and priests, like other public officials, should be chosen by the people. When the Pope objected, the Assembly forced all priests to take an oath of loyalty to the new constitution. Over half the priests in France refused, and Louis supported them. The King had set himself against the revolution.

In the Spring of 1791 the mood in Paris turned nasty.

At Easter the royal family set off from the Tuileries to go to church. But a large and angry crowd refused to let them through the gate. For an hour and three quarters the royal family sat in the coach while people banged their fists on the doors and shouted abuse. Tears of frustration and rage ran down the Queen's face. One soldier shouted at the King, "You are a fat pig. Your appetite costs the people twenty-five millions a year."

Think

● What do people seem so angry about?

73

Escape! June 1791

In the Spring of 1791 the King could see no way out of the trouble over religion. He became more and more worried about the safety of his family. For a long time Marie Antoinette had been secretly planning the royal family's escape from Paris. Louis decided that it was now time to leave. The royal family would head for a town called Montmedy, near France's north-east border. From here the King would get support from foreign armies in the Austrian Netherlands. He would invade France and overturn the Revolution.

On the night of 20 June 1791 the royal family made their daring escape from the Tuileries. At ten o'clock the Queen woke her children. She dressed Louis Charles in a girl's dress and bonnet. The little boy was sleepy and thought that he was being dressed up for a play. Marie Antoinette then sneaked the children out through an unguarded door and into a waiting carriage. Soon afterwards the King and Queen, together with the King's sister and the children's governess, put on their disguises and joined the children.

"When we've got past Chalons," the King said, "we shall be safe". Louis knew that at Somme-Vesle, 14 miles past Chalons, they would meet up with the Duc de Choiseul and forty soldiers who would provide an escort.

It was now that things started to go wrong. The horses fell, causing a break in the harness which had to be repaired. The royal party was now two hours behind schedule. The Duc de Choiseul thought that everything had gone wrong and headed off with his men to Montmedy. When the royal family arrived at Somme-Vesle, there was no escort to meet them.

They pressed on to Sainte-Menehould where they met with more bad luck. For a brief moment the King put his head out of the carriage and the postmaster, a young man called Drouet, who a strong supporter of the Revolution, thought that he recognised Louis's face. When news arrived from Paris that the royal family had escaped, Drouet galloped off after the royal carriage.

The night was moonless, and the carriage passed unnoticed through the dark streets of Paris. At two o'clock it reached the Porte Saint-Martin where the royal party transferred to a bigger, but slower carriage. The carriage travelled at between six and seven miles an hour on the country roads. It would be a two-day journey to Montmedy. By dawn, all was going well and the family began to relax a little.

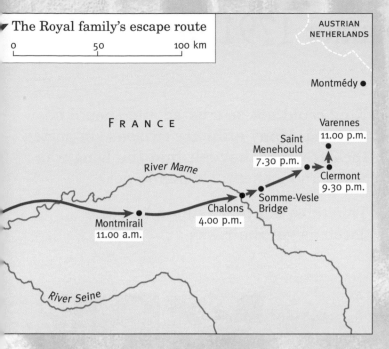

The Royal family's escape route

0   50   100 km

AUSTRIAN NETHERLANDS

FRANCE

Montmédy ●

River Marne

Varennes
11.00 p.m.

Saint
Menehould
7.30 p.m.

Clermont
9.30 p.m.

Somme-Vesle
Bridge

Chalons
4.00 p.m.

Montmirail
11.00 a.m.

River Seine

By the time Louis arrived at the small town of Varennes at 11.00 pm., Drouet was already there. He woke up one of the town officials, a grocer called Sauce, who forced the King's carriage to stop and asked to see passports. The royal party were taken into Sauce's house where Drouet insisted that this was indeed the King and Queen. At six o'clock in the morning, two officials from the National Assembly arrived with orders for the return of the royal family to Paris. Louis said, "There is no longer a king in France."

Think

● Find Chalons, Somme-Vesle and Montmedy on the map.

● What made the escape so risky?

The journey back to Paris was a nightmare. The weather became very hot. Clouds of dust rose from the carriage wheels and clung to the royal family's dirty clothes. Hordes of hostile people surrounded the carriage, shouting insults and spitting. A group of men looked in at the Queen and shouted, "Look at the bitch. It's no good her showing us her child. Everyone knows it isn't his."

After five exhausting days of travelling, the royal family arrived back in Paris. The **National Guard** lined the streets. Huge crowds turned out. Every window in the Champs Elysees was filled with faces. People even climbed onto roofs and trees to get a better view.

But there was a strange silence in the city. The National Assembly had pasted hundreds of offical notices to the walls of Paris reading: 'Whoever applauds the King shall be flogged. Whoever insults him shall be hanged'.

STEP 2

From the autumn of 1789 to the spring of 1791 things began to look much worse for the King. Add these dates, more events and explanations to the chart you began in Step One.

The King is deposed, Summer 1791 to Autumn 1792

The revolutionary leaders in the National Assembly were now divided about what should happen to the King. Many moderate deputies, known as Girondins, still wanted Louis to have a place in France's new constitution. More radical deputies, known as Jacobins, felt that the King could not be trusted and should be deposed. Many ordinary citizens supported the Jacobins. They felt that the King was a liar and a cheat. He had to go!

This table of events shows how the Jacobins got their way.

17 July 1791: The Republican Petition

A large crowd of people gathered in the Champ de Mars in Paris to sign a petition demanding the deposition of the King. The petition was laid out on a kind of altar and people filed past to sign their names. Two men, a hairdresser and an invalid with a wooden leg, were discovered under the steps leading to the altar. Someone accused them of being royalist spies. The crowd dragged the men out and hanged them on the spot. The National Guards were determined to keep order. They fired into the crowd killing about fifty demonstrators.

14 September 1791: The new constitution

The King accepted the new constitution which had been written by the National Assembly. Louis was still allowed to **veto** new laws, but most of his powers were removed. At the ceremony for the new constitution, Louis was forced to sit on a simple chair rather than a throne. The deputies kept their hats on when the King spoke. Louis felt humiliated. When he returned to the Tuileries he slumped into an armchair and cried.

20 April 1792: War declared on Austria

To the east of France was the huge Austrian Empire. It was ruled by the Emperor Leopold, Marie Antoinette's brother. Leopold was protecting nobles who had fled from France and who were plotting against the Revolution. On 20 April 1792, the National Assembly declared war on Austria. But the war started badly France.

20 June 1792: The *sans culottes* attack the Tuileries

The *sans culottes* were working people in Paris who hated the monarchy. They thought that ordinary people like themselves should have power. The *sans culottes* suspected that Louis actually wanted France to lose the war with Austria. On 20 June 1792, a crowd of 8,000 armed *sans culottes* broke into the Tuileries. They forced the King to wear the red cap of liberty and to toast the people of Paris. The mob had spared the King's life, but this was another humiliation for Louis.

25 July 1792: The Brunswick Manifesto

By July 1792 Prussia had joined Austria in the war against France. The leader of the enemy forces was the Duke of Brunswick. On 25 July he signed a document known as the Brunswick Manifesto. This stated that if the Tuileries was attacked again the invading armies would totally destroy Paris. The *sans culottes* were outraged. On the streets of Paris the King and Queen became even more unpopular.

10 August 1792: Massacre at the Tuileries

At the beginning of a boiling hot August, rumours spread that the King was secretly supporting the invading foreign armies. Early in the morning of 10 August, around 10,000 angry revolutionaries from all over Paris marched towards the Tuileries. They broke into the palace and began to butcher the King's soldiers and servants. The royal family fled and took refuge in the sweaty reporters' box at the National Assembly. By evening, the mutilated corpses of over 500 of the King's men were already stinking in the heat.

2-6 September 1792: The September Massacres

At the beginning of September, there was panic in Paris. People feared that the Prussians were about to capture the city. Rumours spread that the priests and nobles in the overcrowded prisons were plotting to escape, kill the citizens of Paris and hand over the city to the Prussians. On 2 September, the *sans culottes* began the brutal murder of the prisoners. The massacre lasted for five days. Nearly 1,500 prisoners were killed. The Revolution had suddenly become much more violent.

21 September 1792: The royal family imprisoned

To most revolutionaries the King now seemed like a useless burden to France. Six weeks after the massacre at the Tuileries a new Assembly (now called the Convention) voted to abolish the monarchy and set up a republic. The people would elect their own rulers and the King would no longer play any part in the government of France. The Convention decided that Louis and his family should be locked away.

STEP 3

From the summer of 1791 to the autumn of 1792, the King had a terrible time. Write the third part of your execution chart.

Trial and execution, December 1792 to January 1793

The royal family in the Temple, a late eighteenth-century engraving

The King and his family spent the autumn of 1792 imprisoned in two storeys of a damp tower in the centre of Paris. It was called the Temple. You can see from this picture that the royal family still had some comforts.

But life in the Temple was not pleasant. The prison guards showed the royal family a lack of respect. They called the King simply 'Louis'. They blew pipe-smoke in the faces of the royal family. Worst of all was the graffiti that the guards scrawled on the walls. One picture showed a stick

Think

- What comforts does the artist show in this picture?

man wearing a crown and hanging from a gibbet; underneath the guard had written, 'Louis taking a bath in the air'. Each day, when the royal family took their afternoon walk in the Temple grounds, hundreds of people gathered outside the Temple and shouted insults at them.

The King had been deposed and imprisoned, but some of the revolutionaries thought that the Convention had not gone far enough. As long as Louis was alive there might be a **counter-revolution**. Some of the Jacobin deputies in the Convention demanded the trial and execution of the King. Their demands gained more support at the end of November when an iron box containing the King's documents was discovered at the Tuileries. It was clear from some of the King's letters in this box that he had been plotting to overthrow the Revolution.

On the morning of 11 December, soldiers arrived at the Temple to escort Louis for trial at the Convention. The King, dressed in a green silk coat, stood before the Convention until the President gave him permission to sit down.

Over thirty charges against Louis were then read out. These included:

- Using force against the National Assembly
- Secretly plotting to overthrow the Revolution
- Accepting the Constitution which he despised
- Attempting to escape from France
- Bankrupting the country

On 4 January the Convention reached its verdict. 693 deputies voted for Louis' guilt. Some deputies were absent, but not one deputy voted for Louis' innocence. The question of the penalty that Louis should pay caused more disagreement. Some deputies wanted the King to be imprisoned for life. Others felt that he should be banished to America. But in the end just over half the deputies thought the King should pay with his life. On 17 January Louis XVI was sentenced to death.

The King was executed on 21 January 1793. The guards in the Temple woke Louis at around 6am. The King dressed in simple clothes. He took off his wedding ring and asked his valet to give it to Marie Antoinette. Louis was placed in a closed carriage and taken through the damp, foggy streets of Paris to the Place de la Revolution. The people lining the streets watched in silence.

The steps to the scaffold were so steep that Louis had to lean on his priest for support. The executioner cut the King's hair roughly. Louis then attempted to address the 20,000 people in the square:

The trial of Louis XVI, an engraving by Giovanni Vendramini, early nineteenth-century

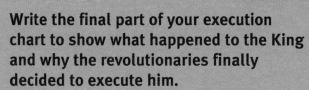

The execution of Louis XVI, late eighteenth-century engraving

"I die innocent of all the crimes of which I have been charged. I pardon those who have brought about my death and I pray that the blood you are about to shed may never be required of France."

But the King's words were drowned out by a roll of drums. The executioner strapped Louis to a plank and pulled the cord on the guillotine. The blade hissed down and sliced through the King's neck. The executioner pulled Louis' head from the basket and showed it, dripping with blood, to the people.

STEP 4

Write the final part of your execution chart to show what happened to the King and why the revolutionaries finally decided to execute him.

Thinking your enquiry through

Now add a conclusion box to your chart. In your conclusion box explain at what point you think the King's death became inevitable.

Compare your conclusion with those of others in your class.

81

Terror!

Why do people still argue about Robespierre ?

Death by guillotine was terrifying – but at least it was quick. The victim was tied face down on a plank of wood about 18 inches wide and four feet long. The top of the plank came to just below the chin. The body was then placed on a bench at the base of the guillotine. The upper part of the guillotine's neck board was lifted and then lowered to hold the victim's neck in place. The victim stared down at a pile of bloody heads in the basket. A cord was pulled. A latch at the top of the guillotine was released. A swish. A thud. The victim's head fell on top of the others in the basket. Blood spurted from the warm neck and splashed the clothes of those who stood too close.

The guillotine was designed by Doctor Joseph Guillotin in 1789. He wanted to introduce a method of execution that was swift, efficient and as painless as possible. Death by guillotine was much quicker than hanging in agony from the end of a gibbet. It was much more humane than being stretched on a cartwheel and beaten to death. On 25 April 1792, the guillotine sliced through the neck of Nicholas Pelletier, a criminal who had committed robbery with violence. The guillotine had claimed its first victim – the first of many thousands.

From the summer of 1793 to the summer of 1794, the guillotine dominated the French Revolution. For over a year, the revolutionary government used the guillotine to execute anyone who was thought to be an enemy of the new Republic. This was the bloodiest and most terrifying phase of the Revolution. It is known as **the Terror**. No-one knows exactly how may people lost their lives during the Terror. Historians have estimated that more than 15,000 people were officially guillotined. But many thousands more were shot, drowned or killed in other ways. Anyone who was not totally loyal to the revolution faced arrest and death.

This man has been linked to the Terror more than any other person. His name was **Maximilien Robespierre.** Robespierre was one of the most important leaders of the Revolution. In 1789 he was elected as a deputy of the Estates General where he made hundreds of speeches arguing for revolutionary changes in France. Robespierre had extreme views about the need for change. He became a leading member of the Convention. This was the new name for the National Assembly. Before long, he was the most important man in France.

Your enquiry

People still argue about Robespierre:

Robespierre was an evil dictator who caused the deaths of tens of thousands of innocent people. He was a ruthless murderer. We should remember him as the butcher of the Revolution.

Robespierre was a politician of great principles. Through every stage of the Revolution he was determined to defend the rights of liberty and equality for French people.

In this enquiry you will find out about Robespierre's character, his ideas, and about the part he played in the Terror. You will collect evidence, so that you can take part in a classroom debate, either attacking or defending Robespierre.

Robespierre's character

This portrait of Robespierre
was painted in 1791.
If we look at the portrait
carefully, and think hard
about what it tells us,
we can find out quite a
lot about Robespierre's
character.

Think

1 Describe Robespierre's face,
clothes and wig.

2 What is Robespierre doing in
this portrait?

3 What do you think this portrait
tells us about Robespierre?

These points of information about Robespierre will help you to
build up a better picture of his character.

1. Robespierre was rather a peculiar man
to look at. He was small and thin. He had
a cat-like face with long lips and grey-
green eyes. He was short-sighted and often
pushed up his tinted glasses onto his
bulging forehead. His skin was pock-
marked and he had a nervous tic. He bit
his nails. Robespierre was very particular
about his appearance. His barber came
every morning to powder his hair. He
chose his clothes very carefully. He walked
very quickly on his high-heeled shoes.

2. Robespierre was born in Arras, a town
in North East France, in 1758. His father
and grandfather were wealthy lawyers. At
first Robespierre had a happy childhood.
But his mother died after the birth of her
fifth child. His father took to drink and
eventually abandoned his children.
Robespierre and his sisters went to live
with their aunts and grandfather.

3. At school, Robespierre was hard-working and intelligent. At the age of eleven he won a scholarship to a famous college in Paris. Robespierre was not one of the brightest students, but he was determined to do well. He spent most of the time studying in his room. He made no close friends and was generally disliked by the other students.

4. In 1780, at the age of 23, Robespierre left his college with a degree in law. He returned to Arras and worked hard to become a successful and respected lawyer. Robespierre earned a reputation as a clever and honest lawyer. He chose to defend poor people who could not pay large fees. He refused to defend people whom he thought were guilty.

5. In 1789 Robespierre was elected to the Estates General. At first he found the speech-making difficult. His voice was weak. Many of the other deputies did not share his extreme views. However, people soon came to admire Robespierre's sincerity and his determination to make France a fairer country. For example, in the early part of the Revolution he tried to abolish the death penalty.

6. Robespierre's life during the early part of the Revolution was dominated by his work as a politician. He was extremely ambitious and was jealous of his rivals. He seemed nervous and highly-strung, but was very aware of his own virtues. Robespierre did not know how to enjoy himself. He had no interest in food or love. He occasionally went to the theatre, but only to see a tragedy.

7. In March 1790, Robespierre was elected President of the Jacobin Club. This made him one of the leading figures of the Revolution. He was determined to fight for the rights of all the French people. But he was disturbed by bloodshed. Some people remarked that he had hidden himself away when the *sans culottes* attacked the Tuileries on 10 August 1792. On the day the King was guillotined he stayed in his room with the shutters closed.

STEP 1

Attackers
1 Choose three really useful facts about Robespierre which could be used to support a negative interpretation of his character.

Defenders
2 Choose three really useful facts about Robespierre which could be used to support a positive interpretation of his character.

Robespierre and the start of the Terror: February – August 1793

In the spring of 1793 Robespierre and the other deputies in the Convention faced three major crises:

Crisis 1: War!

Monarchs in other European countries were horrified by the execution of Louis XVI. They now realised that the only way to prevent the spread of revolution was to join forces with Prussia and Austria. This alliance aimed to destroy the new French Republic. The Convention in Paris decided to strike first. It declared war on Britain and Holland and then on Spain. By March 1793 France was at war with a number of powerful countries. This soon proved disastrous for France. The French forces were defeated by the Austrians on France's north-east border. Robespierre and the other deputies in the convention feared an invasion by France's enemies.

Think

- In what ways could you argue that these crises were partly caused by the actions of the Convention?

Crisis 2: Rebellion!

At the beginning of March 1793, the Convention was horrified to hear of a rebellion in a remote region in the west of France known as the Vendée. The young men in the Vendée were opposed to the Convention's use of conscription to force them into the French army. Many people in the Vendee were also angry at high taxes. Some people wanted the return of their parish priests and of the monarchy. Tens of thousands of people, armed with guns, pitchforks and sickles, attacked the government's soldiers and other republicans in the towns.

Crisis 3: Food shortages!

In the first few months of 1793, food prices began to soar. In order to pay for the war the convention had decided to print huge sums of paper money known as assignats. But as more and more money was printed it became worth less and less. We call this inflation. Rapidly rising prices meant that ordinary people found it hard to afford food and other necessities. Bread became particularly hard to find as farmers did not want to sell their grain for worthless money. People began to question the point of the revolution if the new French Republic could not provide enough food for its citizens. On the streets of Paris the *sans culottes* were becoming more and more restless.

These crises led to a conflict in the Convention between the radical Jacobins and the moderate Girondists. At first these two revolutionary groups had worked together. But, in the spring of 1793, the Jacobins and the Girondists became bitterly divided. The Girondists did not want to introduce price controls. Nor did they share the Jacobin view that property and wealth should be shared out equally among the people. Robespierre, and other Jacobin leaders, blamed the Girondists for the crises facing France. The Jacobins argued that tougher and more extreme policies were needed to save the revolution.

At the beginning of June 1793, the conflict between the Jacobins and the Girondists came to a head. Robespierre urged the sans-culottes, on the streets of Paris, to rise up against the Girondists. On 2 June, 80,000 soldiers and *sans culottes* surrounded the Convention and demanded the arrest the Girondist deputies. Inside one of the Girondists shouted across at a Jacobin "Give him a glass of blood; he is thirsty". The Convention gave in to the demands of the *sans culottes*. Robespierre and the Jacobins now controlled the Convention.

Think

● What do you think the Girondist deputy meant when he said, "Give him a glass of blood; he is thirsty."?

In April 1793, the Convention formed a small group of deputies, called the Committee of Public Safety, to deal with the crises facing France. At first the Girondists controlled this Committee, but from June 1793 the Jacobins were in charge. France was now ruled by this small group of men. Robespierre joined the Committee of Public Safety in July. Although there was no one leader of the Committee, Robespierre soon became its leading member. The government of France was becoming a **dictatorship**.

Robespierre and the other members of the Committee of Public Safety now had the power to do anything they felt was necessary to defend the Revolution. Robespierre said, "The only way to establish a republic is to utterly destroy all opposition". France would now be governed by the guillotine.

STEP 2

Attackers

2 Write a paragraph arguing that Robespierre and the Jacobins should not have taken control of the revolutionary government in the way they did during the spring and summer of 1793.

Defenders

1 Write a paragraph arguing that it was necessary for Robespierre and the Jacobins to take control of the revolutionary government in the way they did during the spring and summer of 1793.

Robespierre and the Terror: September – December 1793

Robespierre never doubted the need for Terror. He believed that the great ideas of liberty and equality were threatened by the enemies of the Revolution. Drastic action was necessary, and Robespierre was prepared to pay the price in human lives.

On the next four pages you will find out about different aspects of the Terror during the autumn of 1793. Use the information on these pages to collect more ideas for your debate.

Attackers

In the debate at the end of the enquiry you will argue that the Terror was an awful waste of human lives. You will also argue that, as the leading member of the Committee of Public Safety, Robespierre was directly responsible for this butchery.

1 For each aspect of the Terror make a note to explain what made it so shocking.
2 Make detailed notes on any aspects which you find particularly terrible.

Defenders

In the debate at the end of the enquiry you will argue that the Terror was necessary. You will also argue that Robespierre cannot be held totally responsible for the brutality of the Terror.

1 For each aspect of the Terror make a note to explain why the Revolutionary Government believed that it was necessary.
2 Make detailed notes when you find evidence that:

Robespierre was not as extreme as some of the other revolutionaries

aspects of the Terror were outside Robespierre's control

Robespierre wanted to make life better for the French people.

Military Terror

The Committee of Public Safety knew that it had to take immediate action to protect the Revolution from foreign armies and from rebellions within France. On 23 August 1793 the Convention issued a **decree** known as the *Levée en Masse*. This forced all French people to take part in the war effort:

- Young, unmarried men were conscripted into the army.
- Married men had to make weapons or to transport food.
- Women were forced to make tents and clothes, or work in hospitals.
- Children had to make bandages.
- Old men were brought to public places to encourage the young men to fight.
- Many men rushed to get married in order to avoid conscription. But anyone who did not obey the *Levée en Masse* was classed as a traitor and could be executed.

Think

- Why do you think that Robespierre and the other members of the Committee of Public Safety thought that the *Levée en Masse* was necessary?

Economic Terror

The Committee of Public safety also took drastic action to solve the crisis of high food prices. Robespierre and some other deputies in the Convention did not want to set limits on the price of food. They thought that the government should not interfere with the economy in this way. But on 5 September the hungry *sans culottes* invaded the Convention and forced the deputies to take action. The Convention passed the Law of General Maximum. This new law:

- set limits on the price of grain and other goods such as salt, meat and wool
- forced farmers and traders to take their goods to market
- introduced the death penalty for any farmer or trader found hoarding grain and other goods.

Think

- Why do you think that the Convention passed the Law of General Maximum when Robespierre and some other deputies were opposed to it?

Religious Terror

For many ordinary people in France it was the brutal attack on the Church which most affected their lives. This attempt to destroy Christianity in France is known as dechristianisation. On 5 October the Convention introduced a new Republican calendar. This new calendar abolished religious holidays and Sundays. Years were no longer dated from the birth of Christ, but from the beginning of the republic (22 September 1792).

All over France, churches were closed, altars were smashed and religious services were banned. Priests were forced out of their parishes and were sometimes made to marry. In some places donkeys were dressed in bishops' robes and led through the streets.

It was the *sans culottes* who were the strongest supporters of dechristianisation. The Convention was simply drawn along with the attacks on religion. Robespierre was particularly shocked by the violence against the Church and tried to get the Convention to stop it. He said, "He who wishes to abolish Christianity is just as fanatical as he who says mass."

Think

- In what ways are the people attacking the church in this picture?

- Why might some people have found this shocking?

An attack on a church during the Terror, a painting by Victor-Henri Juglar, 1880-1885

Political Terror in Paris

In Paris, the *sans culottes* pressed the Committee of Public Safety to take action against people suspected of not supporting the Revolution. On 17 September the Committee passed the Law of Suspects. This new law made it possible to imprison anyone suspected of lacking enthusiasm for the Revolution. Groups of citizens drew up lists of suspects. People went to bed dreading a knock on the door in the middle of the night.

The Paris prisons filled with suspects. The accused people were brought before the Revolutionary Tribunal. This was a special court which was set up to deal with political offences. The Revolutionary Tribunal worked quickly and there was no right of appeal. More and more people were found guilty. The Revolutionary Tribunal had stopped issuing justice – it had simply become a killing machine.

Marie-Antoinette was one of the first people to appear before the Revolutionary Tribunal. Robespierre opposed this 'show trial', but the former queen was executed on 16 October. During the autumn of 1793 nearly 3000 people were guillotined. Many innocent people must have lost their lives alongside those whom the Revolutionary Tribunal considered to be guilty. The following cases are just some of the people who were guillotined on one day:

> Jean Baptiste Henry, aged eighteen, journeyman tailor, convicted of having sawed down a tree of liberty.

> Jean Julien, waggoner, having been sentenced to twelve years hard labour, took it into his head to cry 'Vive le Roi', brought back to the Tribunal and condemned to death.

> Henriette Francoise de Marboeuf, aged fifty-five, convicted of having hoped for the arrival of the Austrians and the Prussians and of keeping provisions for them, condemned to death and executed the same day.

Extracts from the Liste Generale des Condammnes, 1793

A revolutionary tribunal, an eighteenth-century engraving

Political Terror in the provinces

The Committee of Public Safety was determined that the Terror should reach all parts of France. The Committee sent agents known as Representatives-on-Mission, backed by revolutionary armies, into the provinces. The Representatives-on-Mission had the power to arrest anyone they thought was a threat to the Republic. During the autumn of 1793 tens of thousands of people were imprisoned. The shadow of the guillotine fell on town squares across France.

This map shows the main areas of revolt against the revolutionary government. It was in these areas that the Terror was at its most brutal The Committee instructed the Representatives-on-Mission to do anything necessary in order to defeat the rebels.

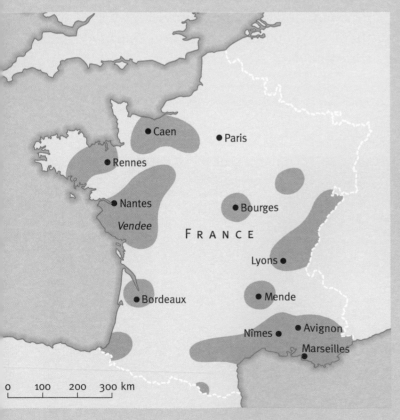

In Lyon, the revolutionary army defeated the rebels in October, but the Committee of Public Safety ordered the Representative-on-Mission, Joseph Fouche, to make an example of France's second city. Robespierre told Fouche that he wanted, "...the worst severity. Humane measures will encourage new conspiracies". Many of Lyon's buildings were set on fire. Hundreds of suspects were arrested. Fouche thought that the guillotine was too slow to execute so many. He had over 300 people blasted to death with cannon.

The attack on Lyon, an eighteenth-century engraving

In the Vendée, the butchery was even worse. The revolt in the Vendée was defeated by the end of 1793, but the Committee of Public Safety ordered the destruction of the whole region as a punishment.

The worst massacre in the Vendée was at Nantes. Here the Representative-on-Mission, Jean-Baptiste Carrier ordered mass drownings on the river Loire. Soldiers took the clothes and belongings of prisoners, tied their hands and feet, and forced them onto barges. The flat-bottomed barges were punched with holes

Think

● Why would
the Committee
of Public
Safety argue
that these
people should
be executed?

which were covered with planks of wood. The barges were pushed out into the centre of the river and the planks were removed. The barges slowly sank and carried their terrified victims to the bottom of the river. More than two thousand people suffered this horrific death. The river became choked with rotting corpses.

The guillotine was also at work. During December the blade fell time and time again in towns throughout the Vendée.

This picture shows four sisters and their mother waiting to be guillotined on 18 December 1793. They were arrested as suspects because they were related to one of the rebel leaders in the Vendée.

The Terror was at its worst in rebel cities like Lyon and Nantes. Other parts of France escaped such terrible butchery and were barely touched by the Terror. But by Christmas 1793, the Terror had claimed the lives tens of thousands of people. And worse was still to come.

Great Terror : spring and summer 1794

Robespierre never doubted the need for Terror, but he always believed that the Terror should be controlled by the Committee of Public Safety. He was worried that some of the Representatives-on-Mission and the revolutionary armies were out of control. In December 1793 the Committee of Public Safety forced some of the Representatives-on-Mission back to Paris and disbanded the revolutionary armies. More and more power was falling into the hands of Robespierre and the other committee members. But, during the spring of 1794, Robespierre faced opposition from two powerful men.

This man was Jacques Hébert. Hébert and his followers (the Hébertists) were more extreme revolutionaries than Robespierre. They were strong supporters of dechristianisation. They also demanded that more people accused of hoarding food should be executed. In March 1793, Hébert organised a mass demonstration to put pressure on the revolutionary government. Robespierre decided that the time had come to destroy him. Hébert and eighteen of his supporters were arrested and guillotined.

This man was George Danton. Danton and his followers were less extreme than Robespierre. They wanted to stop the Terror. Danton saw no need for the Terror to continue now that revolts had been crushed, foreign enemies had been defeated and the economy had recovered. Robespierre feared that ending the Terror could lead to the return of monarchy. Danton had to die. He was not allowed to defend himself at his trial and was executed on 5 April 1794. Passing Robespierre's house on his way to the guillotine, Danton shouted, "You hide in vain, Robespierre. You will follow me."

With Danton's death nothing seemed to stand in Robespierre's way. During June and July 1794 the Terror increased. Robespierre and the Committee of Public Safety stopped the revolutionary tribunals in the provinces and transferred the prisoners to Paris. The prisons were packed, and the Revolutionary Tribunal in Paris could not cope with the number of trials. On 10 June a new law was passed which speeded up the work of the Revolutionary Tribunal. Now almost anyone could be labelled as a 'public enemy', and the Revolutionary Tribunal could only impose one penalty – death.

Think

- What do the deaths of Hébert and Danton tell us about Robespierre's character?

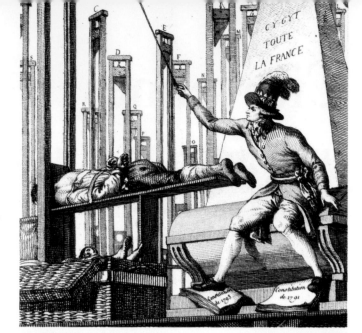

Day after day the executions in Paris continued. During June and July over 1,500 people were beheaded. Robespierre watched none of these people perish. He thought that public executions were too brutal to watch. In the Convention he argued that the Terror was necessary saying, "…if we stop too soon we will die".

The title of this cartoon is 'Robespierre guillotining the executioner after having guillotined all the French people.'

Attackers

Decide what points you will make to attack Robespierre's actions during the spring and summer of 1794.

Defenders

Decide what points you will make to defend Robespierre's actions during the spring and summer of 1794.

During the summer of 1794, many people felt that it was time for the Terror to end. Robespierre'e opponents accused him of trying to set up a dictatorship. On 26 July 1794, Robespierre went to the Convention and made a long and rambling speech attacking his enemies. This was his downfall. The Convention became hostile towards Robespierre and voted for his arrest. On 28 July Robespierre and 21 of his supporters were guillotined. The Terror was dead.

Thinking your enquiry through

It's now time for your debate. The motion is

"Robespierre thoroughly deserves his reputation as the butcher of the Revolution"

Attackers will speak for the motion. Defenders will speak against it. Each side should choose 4 main speakers to cover the 4 parts of the debate:

1 Robespierre's character

2 Robespierre and the start of the Terror

3 Robespierre and the Terror: September-December 1793

4 Robespierre and the Great Terror

If you are a speaker, you will need to use your notes from the steps to help prepare a detailed argument for one part of the debate. If you are not a speaker, you will need to sort out your arguments for each part of the debate so that you can make supporting points and challenge the arguments of your opponents.

Citoyennes

6

What did the French Revolution mean for women?

The artist who painted this picture called it 'The Marriage Contract'. In eighteenth-century France it was common for a woman to provide her husband's family with money, goods or land when she married. This was called a 'dowry'. Before the marriage, families often signed a contract which stated just what the wife's dowry should be. At the front of this painting, on the right, you can see the notary who is writing one of these marriage contracts. In the centre of the painting you can see the young couple who will soon be married. On the left is the woman's family and on the right is the man's family.

Think

● Look carefully at the room where the people are gathered, and at the clothes which the people are wearing. Do you think these people are peasants, urban workers or bourgeoisie?

● Have a good look at the expression on the people's faces, and at the way they are standing or sitting. What can you work out about the attitudes of both families towards the marriage?

● Behind the bride's new mother-in-law, is an open cupboard. It looks like the mother-in-law is expecting some plates, bowls or cups as part of the dowry! Think of a good word to describe the expression on the mother-in-law's face.

● What message do you think the artist wanted to give about marriage in eighteenth-century France?

The young woman in this picture was about to enter a marriage which, in many ways, was very different from marriages today:

1 She would probably live with her husband's family, until her husband could afford a house of his own.

2 Any property which she owned would belong to her new husband once they were married.

3 She would be expected to obey her husband at all times.

4 Even if the marriage was a disaster, divorce would not be allowed.

5 The young woman would be expected to cook, clean, sew and wash clothes for her husband and children.

6 If she worked outside the house she would be paid much less than a man.

7 She was certainly not expected to have views about politics.

Think

● Which aspects of married women's lives in the eighteenth-century France do you find most shocking?

Women in eighteenth-century France were second-class citizens. Nearly everyone accepted that this was the way things were meant to be. Even the great thinkers of the Enlightenment had a traditional view of women. They argued that women only needed enough education to be able to run a good house. This was the way things had always been. This was the way things would always be.

Or was it?

Your enquiry

In this enquiry you will try find out what the Revolution meant for the women of France. What part did women play in the revolution? What did revolutionary women want? How much did the Revolution change women's lives? These are important questions, but they are not easy to answer. Because women were second-class citizens, they have left fewer sources in the archives than men. You will need to use your skills as a historian to squeeze as much as you can out of the sources which you find.

As you work through the enquiry, you will find out about three aspects of women's lives during the French Revolution:

1 Women and the events of 1789.
2 The fight for women's rights, 1790-93.
3 Women and the Terror, 1793-5.

At the end of the enquiry, you will write an article for a history magazine. Your article will explain what the French Revolution meant for women. It will include lots of fascinating details from the sources you have studied. Your article will also explain why we have to be careful in using some of these sources.

Women and the events of 1789

On 5 May 1789 the first meeting of the Estates General took place at the Palace of Versailles. Over a thousand deputies met in the largest hall in the palace.

This is a painting of the first meeting of the Estates General. At the top of the painting, in the shadows, you can just see Louis XVI in his seat. To the King's left sit the 270 noble deputies. To the King's right sit the 291 deputies of the clergy. Facing the King are the 577 deputies of the Third Estate. At the sides, the hall was packed with over two thousand spectators. If you look closely you can see that some of the spectators were women.

Noble women were allowed to watch the Estates General, but not one woman actually took part. It was only **men** who were elected as deputies. In the villages and towns of France, it was nearly always **men** who chose the deputies of the Third Estate. The *cahiers*, which the deputies brought with them to Versailles, were written only by **men**.

Think

- To which estate do you think these women belonged?

98

The points below were all made in a petition which was sent directly to the King on 1 January 1789. All we know about the authors of the petition is that they were 'working women'.

In 1789 women's concerns were ignored, as usual. But some women were determined to be heard!

In the spring of 1789, a small number of women sent petitions to the King explaining what they wanted. Some of these petitions have survived, and they give us some valuable clues about how some women were feeling at the beginning of the Revolution.

1 We do not ask for your permission to send deputies to the Estates General. We prefer to explain our problems directly to you.

2 The women of the Third Estate get a very poor education. They are sent to school with a teacher who hardly knows a word of the Latin. They only attend school until they know enough Latin to read the Mass.

3 Parents often refuse to set up a girl, preferring to spend their money on sons. Women of the Third Estate who have a dowry might marry an artisan or a peasant. Others, with only a small dowry, are obliged to join a convent. Those without a dowry, and without morals, go to the towns and work as prostitutes.

4 We beg you to set up free schools where we might learn our language and be taught, above all, to practise the virtues of our sex: gentleness, modesty, patience, charity. We ask you to give our children a good education, so as to make them subjects worthy of serving you.

5 We ask that men be not allowed to work in women's trades such as seamstresses, embroiderers and millinery shopkeepers. If we are left with the needle and the spindle, we promise never to handle the compass and square. We ask to have work, not to usurp men's authority, but in order to be better regarded by them, and to prevent us from joining the common prostitutes on the street.

Think

- What do the points made by the women in their petition tell us about:

  the problems faced by working women?

  the solutions which they wanted?

- Which phrases and sentences show that the women were making only **limited demands** in their petition to the King?

- Why do you think the working women made only limited demands?

Throughout the summer of 1789, women played an active part in the Revolution. The high price of bread was an important concern for peasants and urban workers. It was the wives of peasants and urban workers who were often involved in rioting when they suspected millers and baker of hoarding grain. Such riots continued into the autumn of 1789. They came to a climax on 5 and 6 October when thousands of women from Paris marched to Versailles to demand bread from the King. This became known as the October Days. You can read about the October Days in more detail on pages.

This picture shows some of the women returning to Paris on 6 October.

Think
- What message does the artist want to give us about the women who were involved in the October Days?
- Why do you think that the October Days was such an important event in the revolution?

In the weeks following the October Days, hundreds of women were interrogated about their involvement in the march to Versailles. Everything these women said was carefully recorded in documents known as 'depositions'.

The deposition on the opposite page is a rich source to use in your magazine article. If you think very carefully, the fascinating details can tell you about the attitudes of some of the women marchers. But there are two main reasons why we have to be careful when using this source:

1 This is only one deposition. We would have to read a lot more depositions to know if the women mentioned in this deposition were typical.

2 To avoid being punished, the women who were interrogated might have tried to describe their actions in a positive way.

Deposition Number 533

Madeline Glain, forty-two years old, a cleaning woman. Wife of Francois Gaillard, an office clerk, with whom she lives at 40 Rue Froidmanteau, in the district of l'Oratoire.

Madeline Glain was forced, as many women were, to follow the crowd that went to Versailles last Monday, 5 October. Having arrived at Sevres, near the porcelain factory, a gentleman asked the women where they were going. They answered that they were going to ask for bread at Versailles. A woman, who Madeline Glain knew to be a prostitute, said that she was going to Versialles to bring back the queen's head, but she was sharply reproached by the others. When they arrived at the streets leading to Versaillles, the same prostitute stopped a Royal Guardsman on horseback, at whom she shouted many insults, threatening him with a rusty sword. The Royal Guardsman said that she was a wretch, and in order to make her release the bridle of his horse which she was holding, he struck her a blow which wounded her arm.

The women arrived at Versailles with the intention of informing His Majesty of the reasons for their march. Madeline Glain's skirts got caught on two spikes of the gate, but the Swiss Guards released her. After that, she went with the other women to the hall of the National Assembly, where they entered, many strong. Some of these women called for the four-pound loaf at eight sols, and for meat at the same price. But Madeline Glain called for silence and said that they were asking that they be not lacking in bread, but not that the price be fixed at that which these women were wanting to have it.

She did not go with the women to Versailles, but returned to Paris carrying the decrees which the women were given at the National Assembly.* The mayor and the representatives of the commune were satisfied and received them with joy. Then Madeline Glain went to the district of l'Oratoire to convey the good news. She cannot give us any information concerning what happened at Versailles on 6 October. However, she learned, without being able to say from whom, that someone named Nicolas, a model in the academy, on that day, Tuesday, had cut off the heads of two Royal Guards who had been massacred by the people. Since then Nicolas has not reappeared in the district.

(* The **decrees** were orders from the Assembly which stated that the people of Paris should be supplied with bread.)

Think

- In what ways was Madeline Glain more moderate in her actions than the prostitute she was with on the way to Versailles?

- In what ways was Madeline more moderate than some of the other women who entered the National Assembly?

- How did Madeline Glain's actions on 6 October show that she was more moderate than some of the other marchers?

- What do you think the following people wanted from the march to Versailles:
  - Madeline Glain?
  - The prostitute?
  - Some of the women with extreme views who entered the National Assembly?

It's time to make detailed notes for your magazine article.

1 Write detailed notes for the introduction, using the information on pages 96 to 101.

- Explain what aspects of women's lives in eighteenth century we might find most shocking today.

- Explain what your article is about.

2 Write detailed notes for the first section of your article. This should be about women's actions and attitudes in 1789. Your notes should explain:

- How women got involved in the Revolution.

- What exactly the revolutionary women seemed to want.

- The ways in which some women made only limited demands in 1789.

3 Remember to include fascinating details from the sources you have used. You may want to select particular quotes from the sources. Make sure that you link the details and quotes from the sources to one of the points in your notes.

4 Finally, when you use a source, make sure you make a note of how the source was produced, and any problems which historians face in using it.

The fight for women's rights, 1790-1793

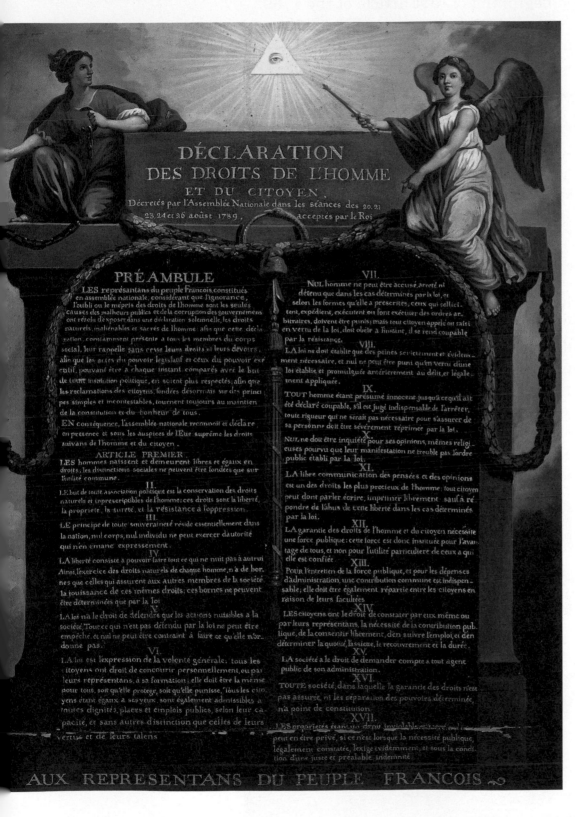

DÉCLARATION
DES DROITS DE L'HOMME
ET DU CITOYEN,
Décretés par l'Assemblée Nationale dans les séances des 20.21
23.24 et 26 août 1789, acceptés par le Roi

This is a painting of one of the most important documents of the French Revolution. On 26 August 1789 the National Assembly issued **The Declaration of the Rights of Man and the Citizen**. The Declaration set out how French people should live in future. It was based on the two important beliefs of the Revolution: **liberty** and **equality**.

Think

- Which of the two important beliefs do you think the woman on the left represents? What makes you think this?

- Look very carefully at the painting and make a list of all the ways in which the artist tried to make the Declaration look special.

The revolutionaries used a woman to symbolise their belief in liberty, but the Declaration itself did little to change women's lives. Just compare the beginning of first article of the 1789 Declaration with the beginning of first article of the Universal Declaration of Human Rights, made by the United Nations in 1948:

1789 Declaration of the Rights of Man and the Citizen
"Men are born and remain free and equal in rights..."

1948 Universal Declaration of Human Rights
"All human beings are born free and equal in dignity and in rights..."

Think

- How are the two articles similar?
- How are the two articles different?

The Declaration of the Rights of Man and the Citizen said nothing about the rights of women (just as it said nothing about the rights of men who worked for wages and did not own property). But this did not stop women arguing for equality with men. In Paris, some revolutionary clubs now began to allow women to attend their meetings. Women also set up political clubs of their own. The women in these clubs wrote pamphlets and made speeches demanding equal rights with men. **The campaign for women's rights had begun!** This picture shows a meeting of the Patriotic Club for women revolutionaries.

Think

- Do you think these women are peasants, urban workers or bourgeoisie?
- What do the women seem to be doing at their meeting?

One of the boldest campaigners for women's rights was Marie Gouge. Marie was a self-educated butcher's daughter from the south of France. When the Revolution began, Marie was writing pamphlets and plays using the pen name of Olympe de Gouges. In 1791 she decided to use her skill as a writer to attack the deputies of the National Assembly who had forgotten the women in their Declaration. Olympe de Gouges wrote **The Declaration of the Rights of Woman**.

These are five of the articles from The Declaration of the Rights of Woman. The language which Olympe used is tricky to understand, so we have provided a summary of each article in the column on the left. (But we have jumbled them up.)

Think

● See if you can match each article to the correct summary.

Article 1
Woman is born free and remains equal to man in rights.

Article 6
The law should be the expression of the general will. All citizenesses and citizens should take part, in person, or by their representatives, in its formation.

Article 10
No-one should be disturbed for his fundamental opinions; woman has the right to mount the scaffold, so she should have the right equally to mount the rostrum, provided that these manifestations do not trouble public order as established by law.

Article 13
Taxation of women and men is equal; she takes part in all ...painful taxes; she must therefore have the same proportion in the distribution of places, employments, offices, dignities and in industry.

Article 17
Property belongs to both sexes whether united or separated; it is for each of them an inviolable and sacred right.

A
Women and men pay the same taxes, so they should have the same job opportunities.

B
Women, like men, should be able to vote for those who make the laws.

C
Women should be allowed to speak their minds

D
Women should be allowed to keep their own property

E
Women and men should have equal rights

We can try to find out if the campaign for women's rights had any success by looking at the ways in which life in France changed during the first two years of the Revolution.

After 1789, the deputies in the National Assembly passed new laws which tried to make France a fairer country. Here is a summary of the changes. Campaigners for women's rights were very keen to see how the changes affected them.

Changes introduced by the National Assembly

Changes in government

1 The deputies of the new Assembly were to be elected every two years by 'active' citizens. The 'active' citizens were men who paid more than the minimum amount of tax.
2 France was divided into 83 Departments, each run by an elected council.
3 'Active' citizens had the right to elect local councillors, judges and tax-collectors.

Social changes

1 Jobs were to be allocated on the basis of merit (but only to men).
2 Women and men were allowed to sue for divorce.
3 Torture and hanging were abolished, and everyone had a right to trial by jury.
4 Girls were granted equal rights to the inheritance of family property.

Changes in the Church

1 Church lands were sold and the money was used to pay off France's debts.
2 The tithe (church tax) was abolished.
3 Priests were to be elected by 'active' citizens.

Economic changes

1 Customs barriers inside France were introduced.
2 Unfair taxes were abolished and new taxes were introduced, based on the ability to pay.
3 A paper currency, the *assignat*, was introduced. The *assignats* could be used to buy church lands.

Think

- Which of these changes do you think the campaigners for women's rights might have been **particularly pleased** about?

- Which of these changes do you think the campaigners for women's rights might have been **angry** about?

- Overall, why do you think these changes were disappointing for the campaigners for women's rights?

Women never gained the same political rights as men during the French Revolution. Women were not allowed to hold office, nor were they allowed to vote. The revolutionary government continued to treat women as second-class citizens. By the autumn of 1793, many deputies had become unhappy at the idea of women expressing their views in the women's clubs. On 30 October 1793, the revolutionary government banned all women's clubs. Four days later, Olympe de Gouges was sent to the guillotine.

STEP 2

It is time to make detailed notes for the second part of your magazine article. This part should be about the campaign for women's rights, 1790-93. Your notes should cover these aspects:

1 How some women began to demand equal rights with men.

2 What exactly these women seemed to want.

3 The extent to which the campaigners for women's rights were successful.

To back up your notes on what some women seemed to want, you may want to select details and quotes from Olympe de Gouge's Declaration of the Rights of Woman. Make sure that you link the details and quotes to the points in your notes. You may wish to make background notes on Olympe de Gouges and her Declaration.

I like the way the author has quoted from the sources.

Women and the Terror

In the spring of 1794 Harlay Ducroquet wrote this letter to her son:

Damiens, this fourth of Ventose, Year two of the Republic

My son,

I write to let you know that tomorrow, or the day after tomorrow, I will send off a small package of old things for your children. I wanted to have something better; for the moment, I have nothing else. The postage will be paid. As for me, I am not doing very well. Good food is unavailable. There is nothing to be had. To get four eggs you have to queue with six hundred people and wait your turn, and for everything, generally. They say nothing about soap either, except that there will not be any more. You have to stay filthy for the lack of it.

One of my cousins brought me a little cake. I send you a piece. It will be a bit hard, but you can heat it up. You will find several books that I am sending back to you. In one you will find a ten-livre note. Three livres of this comes from Sophia for your pomade and the money for your bottle. The rest is for your children. This book will be tied up with string. Look out for it. Let me know, I beg you, when you have received it at Citoyenne Roucoult's address, and don't delay, because I'll be uneasy.

I saw in the paper that someone named Ducroquet was arrested. I'll admit to you that I can't stop thinking about it, although I know full well that you are a good patriot. This name Ducroquet caught my eye, but I was told that it was a deputy in the assembly. Let me have some news of you. That would give me pleasure, as I think you know. I send you my love, and I am,

Your mother, Harlay Ducroquet.

Harlay Ducroquet's letter gives us a fascinating glimpse of the difficulties which women faced during the years of the Terror. As food became scarce, women found it more and more difficult to feed their families. At the same time, women lived in fear that their loved ones would be arrested, imprisoned and guillotined. Ordinary women who complained about food shortages, or who criticized the authorities, faced arrest themselves.

Think

- How do we know that Harlay Ducroquet was not a poor woman?
- What difficulties did Harlay Ducroquet face in the spring of 1794?
- Why was Harlay Ducroquet particularly concerned about her son?

In fact, the man, whose arrest Harlay had read about in the newspaper, **was** her son. He went to the guillotine a few weeks later.

In September 1794 Anne Guinee was imprisoned after she had insulted a local official, while standing in a queue at a food market. After spending 17 days in prison, she was eventually released on bail. Anne then wrote a petition to the revolutionary leaders of her commune. She asked for work, and for a speedy judgement about her case. This extract from Ann Guinee's petition gives us some interesting details about women's actions and attitudes during the Terror.

Think

- What difficulties did Anne Guinee face in the autumn of 1794?

- In what ways did Anne Guinee show that she was a determined and brave woman?

- In what ways did Anne Guinee hold traditional views about her role as a woman?

This 25 Fructidor, Second Year of the French Republic.

Citizens

I, citoyenne Anne Felicite Guinee, twenty-four years old, married to Citizen Fillastre, a wig-maker, on Rue des Vieilles Auduette, inform you that I was arrested on 22 Germinal, at the place des Droits de l'Homme, where I had gone to get butter.

For a long time I have had to feed my family on bread and cheese and, tired of complaints from my husband and my boys, I was compelled to go and queue to get something to eat. For three days I had been going to the same market without being able to get anything, despite the fact that I had waited from 7 or 8 am to 5 or 6 pm.

After the distribution of butter on 22 Germinal, a citizen came over to me and said that I was in a very delicate condition. To that I answered, "You can't be delicate and be on your legs for so long. I wouldn't have come if there were any other food". He replied that I needed to drink milk. I answered that I had men in my house who worked, and that I couldn't nourish them with milk. I told him that he was an imbecile.

Here, on the spot, I was arrested and brought to the guard-house. I wanted to explain myself, but I was silenced and dragged off to prison. About 7 pm I was led to the Revolutionary Committee where I was called a counter-revolutionary, and was told I was asking for the guillotine because I told them I preferred death to being treated in the terrible way they were treating me. I asked to write to my husband. I was refused.

By the spring of 1795, the food shortages had become even worse. Bread was strictly rationed. There were riots in many parts of France. In May the government lowered the bread ration to just two ounces a day. The citizens of Paris could not survive on this.

On 20 May, thousands of *sans culottes*, armed with guns, pikes and swords, attacked the Convention. The women marched in front as they believed that the government's soldiers would never open fire on them. The crowd of women and men burst through the doors of the Convention shouting for food they could afford. Some of the deputies scrambled to the higher benches, out of harm's way.

When the government gained control, it arrested many of the rioters. The police interrogated the accused people. The document shown here is a record of one of the police interrogations of a suspected female rioter called Vigniot. We need to be careful - this example may not be typical, and any accused woman would want to downplay her part in the violence. However, the source contains some really interesting details about women's actions and attitudes on 20 May.

Think

● What do you think the police interrogation was trying to prove?

● Vigniot claimed that she was not a leader of the rioters. Even if this was true, how do her answers show that women played an important role in the attack on the Convention?

Q *Why aren't you wearing the clothes appropriate for your sex?*

A The trade I am in does not allow it, as women's clothes would constrain me in working.

Q *On 1 Prairial (20 May) weren't you leading some women, and didn't you have an open saber in your hand?*

A No.

Q *On 2 Prairial , weren't you also leading some women who went to the Convention?*

A As I was going to work around 6 am on the day in question, I was taken there by force, by some women from Faubourg Marceeau. I was obliged to march with them, and I left them near the Champs-Elysees

Q *Didn't you go with the women to the Convention?*

A No

Q *When you left the Faubourg with these women, didn't you have an unsheathed saber in your hand?*

A I had a saber in my hand, but it was in a scabbard.

Q *At what time did you leave these women?*

A I left them at around 1pm.

Q *Where did you go after she left them?*

A I went to drink a pint of wine at the cabaret at the waterfront near Pont-Marie. I was with a young woman and a single girl.

Q *Do you know the names of these two women?*

A I do not.

It is time to make detailed notes for the final part of your magazine article. This should be about women and the Terror, 1793-95. Your notes should explain:

1 The difficulties which women faced during the Terror.

2 Women's involvement in the attack on the Convention on 20 May 1795.

Remember to include interesting details from the sources you have used. You may want to select particular quotes from the sources. Make sure that you link the details and quotes from the sources to one of the points in your notes.

Finally, when you use a source, make sure you make a note of how the source was produced and any problems which historians face in using it.

What illustrations shall we use!

Thinking your enquiry through

Use the detailed notes you have made to produce your magazine article about what the French Revolution meant for women. The editor has asked you to set out your article across three pages of the magazine.

Page 1 Introduction. Women and the events of 1789

Page 2 The fight for women's rights, 1793-5

Page 3 Women and the Terror.

In each section you will need to explain women's actions and attitudes during this phase of the revolution. You can make your article really interesting by including the carefully-chosen details and quotes from the sources you have studied.

You can introduce these details and quotes like this:

> An example of the kinds of difficulties which women faced during the Terror is found in the letter of Harlay Ducroquet to her son in the spring of 1794. The mother wrote, ' Good food is unavailable. There is nothing to be had. In order to get four eggs....'

The editor has asked you to suggest an illustration for each section of your article. You can either choose a real picture or ask for one to be drawn. For each illustration, make sure you explain why you have chosen it and how it will make your article even better.

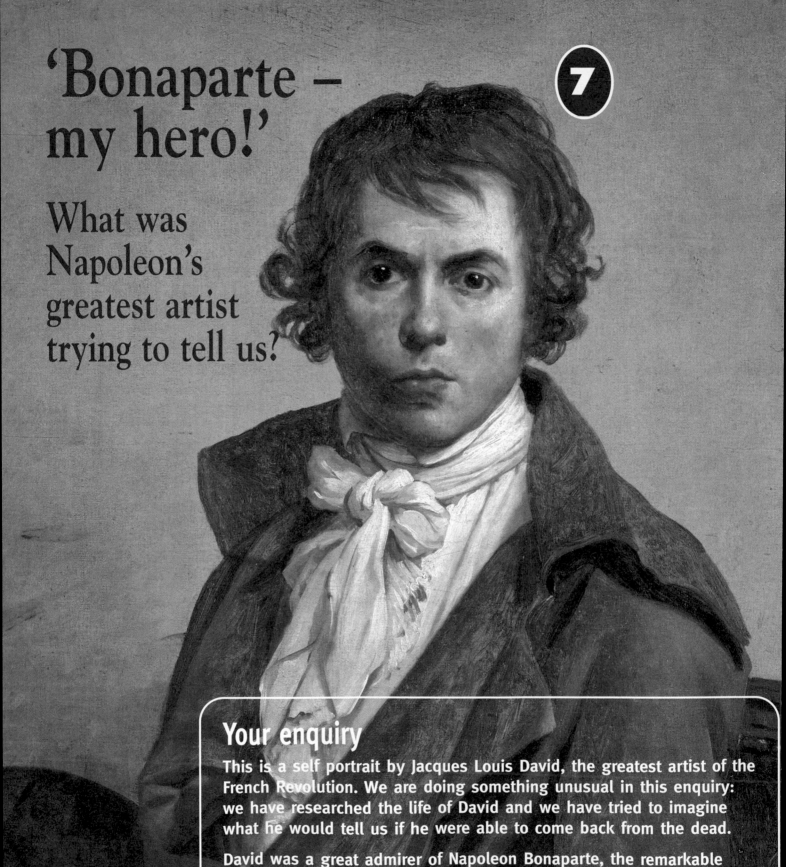

'Bonaparte – my hero!'

What was Napoleon's greatest artist trying to tell us?

Your enquiry

This is a self portrait by Jacques Louis David, the greatest artist of the French Revolution. We are doing something unusual in this enquiry: we have researched the life of David and we have tried to imagine what he would tell us if he were able to come back from the dead.

David was a great admirer of Napoleon Bonaparte, the remarkable soldier who ruled France from 1799 to 1815. As you work through the enquiry you will learn what Napoleon achieved and how David showed his admiration for Napoleon in his paintings. At the end, there is a challenge for you, but first let's read what David has to say...

Greetings. My name is Jacques Louis David. The authors of your book describe me as the greatest artist of my day – and they arc right! In this enquiry you will read my words and read my paintings. They will tell you my own story and the story of the greatest Frenchman who ever lived: Napoleon Bonaparte.

Before Bonaparte

Before I talk about Napoleon, I will tell you about the years from 1789 to 1794 when so much changed in my life – and so much changed in France.

Before the Revolution, I had already won fame by painting scenes from ancient history. I loved to show brave, **patriotic** men and women who were prepared to die for their beliefs. When the Revolution broke out, I was delighted. My own people in my own day were standing up for freedom against the **tyranny** of kings.

In 1793 my friend Robespierre took control after the death of King Louis XVI. He asked me to use my artistic gifts to help the Revolution. He knew I could not make great speeches. I had a horrible growth inside my mouth which gave me an awful speech impediment. When I made speeches people laughed. But when I showed my paintings, they gasped in admiration.

In July 1793, one of our great republican leaders, Jean-Paul Marat, lay in his bath, working on some papers. Charlotte Corday, a young woman, tricked her way in to see him and plunged a knife into his chest. This was her revenge for the execution of the King. When I unveiled my famous painting of this hero's death, I told the leaders of the revolution:

"It is to you colleagues, that I offer the tribute of my brushes. When gazing at Marat's vivid and blood-soaked features you will recall his virtues which must never cease to be your own"

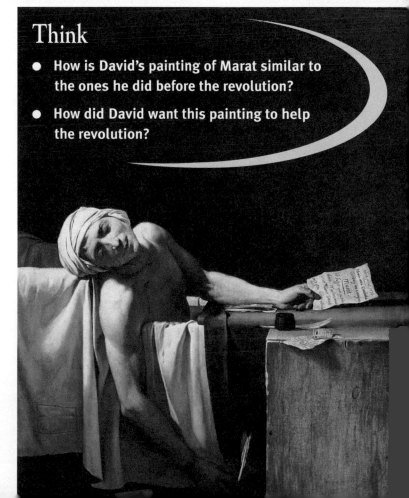

Painting was not the only way to spread messages about the greatness of the Revolution. Before Marat was buried, I organised a public display of his corpse. By then the body had gone stiff, but I ordered the embalmers to cut and rearrange his body to sit in a bath, just as it was when he died. Unfortunately his arm fell off when a spectator went too close, but otherwise everything went well. Thousands of people never forgot the day they saw a hero of the Revolution.

Think

- Look at this print of the Festival of the Supreme Being. What examples can you find of David's planning?

- How high do you think the man-made mountain is?

I had even more success with my street festivals. When Robespierre set up France's alternative religion, I organised one of my greatest ceremonies, the 'Festival of the Supreme Being'. I designed costumes in the red, white and blue of our new *tricolore* flag. I made a huge mountain from plaster and cardboard on which was planted a fully-grown tree. This symbolised the liberty of France. I also designed carriages, street decorations, statues and massive monuments. The people flocked onto the streets to join in these great 'fetes' which made them feel good about the Revolution.

I even published one or two rude cartoons. This one mocks our enemy, the King of England. He is shown as the devil's backside, 'showering' his

people with taxes. My cartoons were not great art … but they strengthened French pride in the Revolution.

I was using my art to spread Robespierre's message far and wide. There is a word for this – **propaganda**. By 1794 I was the propaganda master of the Revolution. But it did not last.

In the summer of 1794 Robespierre's enemies decided that he was taking too much power. It was clear that they wanted to destroy Robespierre, his ideas and his friends – including me. It was at this point that I painted the self portrait you saw on page 112. Maybe you can now understand the look in my eye!

Sure enough, in July 1794 Robespierre was arrested and sent to the guillotine. I found myself in prison, wondering what – if anything – the future held for me.

1 What does David mean when he calls himself the "propaganda master of the revolution".

2 Make a list of methods used by David to spread propaganda about the French Revolution

3 Make a list of methods that David could have used to spread propaganda if he had been alive in our own day.

A new hero

I was lucky. The new government released me in 1795. I went back to painting while our new rulers tried – and failed – to bring peace to France.

These were difficult years. Revolutionaries and royalists continued to struggle for power at home. At the same time, almost every other country in Europe was at war with France as they tried to put a stop to our Revolution.

In October 1795 a brave young soldier crushed a dangerous royalist revolt in Paris. He quickly became one of France's leading generals. His name was Napoleon Bonaparte.

In 1796 and 1797 Napoleon's army won some remarkable victories against our Austrian enemies. He returned to Paris as a hero. At a dinner party Napoleon rearranged the place names at the dining table so that we could sit next to each other. During the meal he invited me to paint his portrait. I was proud to accept.

Soon afterwards Napoleon came to my studio. He could not bear to sit still as I painted him. He was restless, a man of action. In the end I could only paint his head – but as I wrote at that time …

"What a fine head he has. It is pure. It is great. Here is a man to whom altars would have been built in ancient times. Yes my friends … Bonaparte is my hero!"

115

Soon after I painted his portrait, Napoleon sailed with his army to Egypt. He hoped to weaken Britain by cutting her trade routes to India. While he was away things went badly wrong in France. By 1799, the country was in debt, there were food shortages, and other generals had lost important battles in Italy. It looked as though France was about to collapse.

Reports of all these problems reached Napoleon in Egypt. He made his way back to Paris. In November 1799 he took some loyal soldiers to the Assembly and forced the politicians to hand all power over to him. This sort of quick, small-scale use of force to change a government is called a *Coup d'etat*. It was illegal – but I am sure it was what France needed.

Let me show you someone else's propaganda. This English cartoon was made in 1799. It shows Napoleon and his troops as crocodiles who have just returned from the river Nile. They are threatening to gobble up the poor little French politicians in the Assembly. You English have always enjoyed calling us frogs.

Think

- How can you tell this cartoon was made by Napoleon's enemies?

- Why do you think one crocodile has a crown on his head?

- Why was David pleased when Napoleon took power by force?

After this *Coup d'Etat*, Napoleon held the title of First Consul of France. In theory he shared power with two more consuls ... but he was clearly in charge. He organised a **plebiscite** to ask France's nine million voters whether they approved of this new arrangement. 3 million voted in favour and only 1,500 voted against.

Within months of taking power, Napoleon lifted the spirits of his people by success on the battlefield. In 1800, he led an army over the Alps and into Italy where he defeated the Austrians at the battle of Marengo. With Napoleon at the height of his powers, we were sure Napoleon was leading us all to greatness and glory.

In 1800, the King of Spain asked me to paint a portrait of Bonaparte leading his army into Italy. This time, Napoleon refused to sit for me but he told me to paint him "calm on a fiery horse". He said that the exact truth did not matter in a painting – after all, he had really crossed the Alps on a mule! All that mattered, he said, was that I should capture a sense of his genius.

I did my best. In 1801 I finished this portrait of our great new leader.

This fine painting is also a piece of propaganda about Napoleon's leadership.

From the section 'A new hero', list some ways in which Napoleon had shown his leadership qualities by 1800.

Explain how David has tried to capture Napoleon's leadership qualities in this painting.

Reformer and Emperor

After defeating the Austrians at Marengo in 1800, Napoleon turned his attention to problems at home. He set about a series of reforms. Many of them surprised some of us.

Think

- How might some of these reforms surprise David? (You may find it helpful to compare this table with the one on page 106).

What Napoleon did	Why he did it
In 1801, Napoleon signed a **Concordat** (agreement) with the Pope. This said that France rejoined the old Roman Catholic Church. But … • The French government, not the Pope, chose the Bishops and paid the clergy. • No one paid **tithes** • No one had to return any church property taken during the revolution	Napoleon called religion the "cement of social order". He knew that millions of French people missed the hope and security the old Church gave them. Napoleon also knew that priests would encourage people to do what the government wanted. After all, the government now paid priests' wages!
Napoleon allowed people in each area of France to elect local councils – but real power lay with local prefects, chosen by the government in Paris. Napoleon also used the army and special courts to end the threat of local bands of robbers.	Napoleon wanted the people who ran local government to be of good quality – and to do what he wanted. The prefects quickly improved law and and gave people peace in their home area.
Between 1800 and 1808, Napoleon led a group of experts in removing or replacing old and foolish laws. The new laws were called the Code Napoleon. Men kept many rights that they had won during the revolution – but women's rights were cut.	Napoleon wanted government to be clear and efficient wherever he had power. The Code Napoleon was used in every part of France and in all the lands he conquered throughout Europe.
Napoleon set up a Ministry of Police, which had a network of spies all over France. It also **censored** newspapers, books and plays.	Napoleon wanted to know exactly what people were thinking and doing – especially as France was at war with so many enemies.
Napoleon introduced The Legion of Honour (1802). This system of titles rewarded the achievements of talented men. He created about 3000 new nobles and gave awards to politicians, soldiers and artists.	Napoleon wanted to encourage people to be loyal to their country and their leader by offering titles as rewards.
Napoleon organised a massive building project to improve roads, canals and public monuments.	Roads and canals improved trade and helped Napoleon to move and supply his armies.
Napoleon introduced new schools called Lycées. These concentrated on subjects such as maths, science and history rather than Latin and Greek. Napoleon said that "women were not suited to being educated".	The Lycées were designed to produce many educated young men who would serve France loyally in the army and the government.

Some of these reforms took years to carry out, but, quite quickly, law and order improved and so did trade and employment. It was as if Napoleon was heaven-sent. He was healing our nation after all the pain and confusion since 1789. By another plebiscite in 1802, the voters made him first consul for life.

Let me show you another painting. This one was not made by me but by one of my best pupils, Antoine-Jean Gros. It is based on an incident from Napoleon's wars in Egypt. The painting is called 'Napoleon visiting the plague victims of Jaffa'. Once again the actual event shown in this painting never happened. My student Gros just wanted to paint a scene that summed up what Napoleon's power and personality could do for France.

The figure of Napoleon in this painting reminds me that Robespierre had once warned us that one day a soldier may take over the Revolution. He said we should watch out for a "**Messiah** in army boots". Some began to worry that we may be giving Napoleon too much power.

Think

- Which figures are the plague victims?

- What is Napoleon doing?

- How does this painting fit with Robespierre's words about a "Messiah in boots"?

- What is the artist trying to tell us about what Napoleon was doing for France?

In 1804 Napoleon announced that he wished to become Emperor of France. Was he betraying everything we had fought for? Marat had died for his part in the execution of our king. I had painted him as a hero. Now my new hero Bonaparte was taking a crown. What did it all mean for France?

I was puzzled but I could not bring myself to oppose Napoleon. After all, he was restoring greatness and glory to France and, in another plebiscite, a massive majority of voters said they wanted him to become Emperor.

Think

● Why was David troubled at Napoleon becoming Emperor?

● Why do you think David decided not to oppose Napoleon?

The coronation took place on 2 December 1804. Napoleon asked me to organise the processions, the colour schemes, the decoration of the cathedral and the positioning of all our rich and powerful visitors. And he wanted each famous face to appear in a massive painting of the coronation: the largest to have been made in Europe for hundreds of years – it was to be seven metres by ten!

Here is my masterpiece. I chose to capture the moment when Napoleon took the crown and placed it on the head of his wife Josephine. He had already placed the crown of laurels on his own head. The Pope sat behind him … but he did very little. Napoleon allowed the Pope to give a blessing but insisted that he must not actually crown the new Emperor or Empress. That would be to suggest that the Pope had more power than Napoleon.

Gathered around are members of Napoleon's family, nobles from the Legion of Honour, soldiers, church leaders and politicians. I cheated a little: I included Napoleon's mother sitting with the best view of all – even though she did not attend. I made Josephine look much younger than she was. Some nobles complained that they could not be seen so I had to move their position. I placed myself in the picture – and can you find the young altar boy who has lost concentration and is admiring the sword of a soldier?

Think

● In the picture, find …
  – Napoleon
  – the Pope
  – Josephine
  – Napoleon's mother
  – David, sitting with his sketch book open

● Why do you think nobles worried about where they were placed in the painting?

● Why do you think David showed the altar boy looking at a sword?

As I watched, I knew that this scene was exactly like the court of an old-fashioned king. Was the Revolution dying? My worries eased a little when Napoleon took the bible and swore this oath:

"I swear to maintain the territory of the French Republic; to respect and enforce the laws of the Concordat and freedom of worship; to respect and enforce equality before the law, political and civil liberty; to impose no tax except according to law; to maintain the Legion of Honour; and to govern only in accordance with the interests, the happiness and the glory of the French people".

STEP 3

From the section 'Reformer and Emperor', list some ways in which Napoleon changed France between 1799 and 1804

The paintings by David (above) and Gros (page 119) try to show how Napoleon is a man of great power. Which painting do you think does this best and how does the artist achieve it?

121

Conqueror of Europe

Three days after the coronation, Napoleon called thousands of his troops to gather before their new emperor in Paris. He gave each regiment its own flag or standard. Above the flag was an eagle.

The Emperor stood on a platform and proclaimed:

> Soldiers, here are your flags! These eagles will be wherever your Emperor deems them necessary to defend his throne and his people. You will swear to defend them with your life and to uphold them constantly by your courage on the road to victory. Do you swear?

The soldiers raised their standards towards Napoleon as their chorus rang out – "We swear!" It was a dramatic moment. The Emperor asked me to capture it in another painting. It is a symbol of the total loyalty and enthusiasm that Napoleon could inspire in his troops.

I must be honest and tell you that I am not happy with this painting. Napoleon angered me by interfering. I had painted a winged goddess of victory above the soldiers – but he thought this was foolish and told me that it must removed.

What made matters worse was that he was so slow to pay me for all my magnificent work. You may not be surprised to hear that this was the last picture I ever painted for the Emperor.

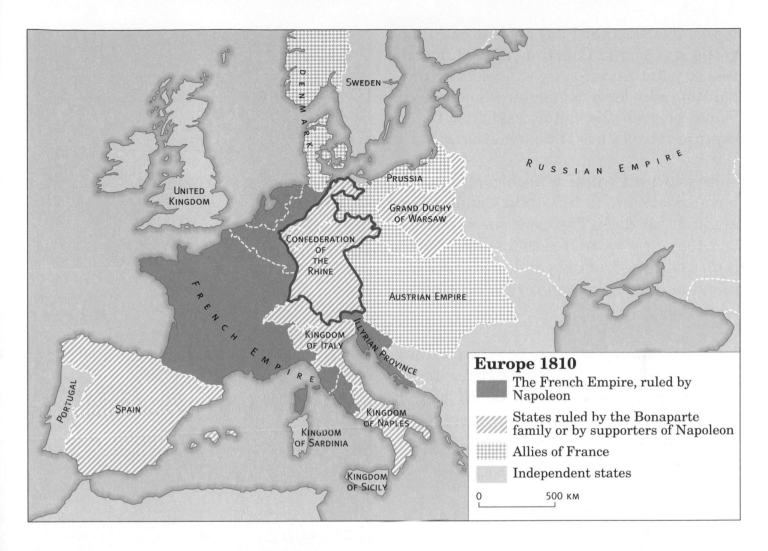

Europe 1810

■ The French Empire, ruled by Napoleon

▨ States ruled by the Bonaparte family or by supporters of Napoleon

▧ Allies of France

□ Independent states

0 ———— 500 KM

In the years that followed, Napoleon led his armies to victory all over Europe. I admit that he could never defeat you British because your navy always protected you, but by 1810 he controlled Europe from Spain in the west to the borders of Russia in the east.

Napoleon took some lands and made them part of the French Empire. He placed others under the control of members of his own family. Some nations saw there was no point in resistance and chose to become allies of France. Europe had seen nothing like this since the days of the mighty Roman Empire.

Wherever Napoleon's victories gave him sufficient control, he spread his own ideas. Taking France as the model, he worked tirelessly to control the power of the Church, to end **feudalism** and to give people rights they had never known before. In many places his Code Napoleon became the basis of law. His dream was that there should be one, united Europe. In 1811 he said:

> I want to finish a job that has just begun. We need a European court of appeals, one currency, one system of weights and measures and a code of law. It must make the peoples of Europe into one nation.

It was in 1812 that I did my last painting of the great man. This time though, I was free to paint him exactly as I wished. The painting was for a Scotsman who admired Napoleon and who simply asked me to capture the essence of his greatness.

Here is what I painted. Look carefully. I have shown him in his study. Candles are alight at his desk. The clock shows that it is 4.13am. He wears his soldier's uniform and is turning from his desk. He is about to put on his sword and review his troops on parade.

Napoleon himself came to see the painting. He admired it greatly and congratulated me. "You have found me out, dear David; at night I work for my subjects' happiness and by day I work for their glory".

Think

● What do you think Napoleon meant by this comment to David?

● David knew that this painting would be seen in Britain. Why do you think he decided not to show Napoleon in battle?

Later that same year Napoleon wrote this about himself:

It is said that I love power. Well, has anyone any reason to complain? Never have the prisons been so empty; the roads have never been safer. The government is strong, my hand is steady and officials do their job properly. All citizens and all their properties are well-protected. I have governed for the people and their interests.

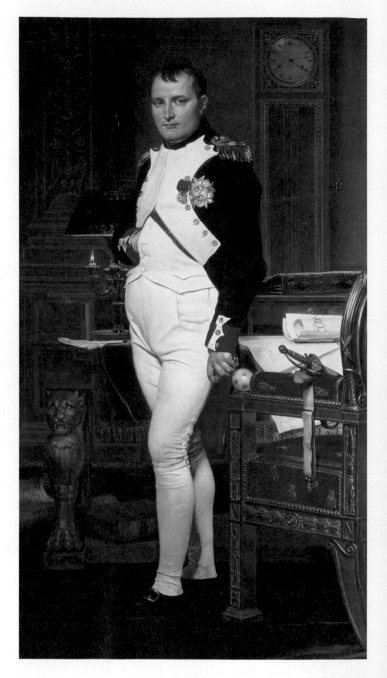

STEP 4

Explain what David was trying to say about Napoleon in this painting.

In your explanation refer to details in the painting and to information about Napoleon from the section "Conqueror of Europe".

Injury and insult

That year – 1812 – was the beginning of the end for Napoleon. I will spare you the details of his downfall. In 1815 your British army under the Duke of Wellington defeated him at the Battle of Waterloo. You sent our great emperor to the tiny island of St Helena in the middle of the Atlantic Ocean. He died there in 1821 at the age of 51.

I left France forever. I moved across the border to Belgium. Not long before my death in 1825, the Duke of Wellington had the nerve to ask me to paint his portrait. I replied:

> I have not almost reached the age of 70 just to dirty my palette. I would rather cut off my own hand than paint an Englishman. I do not paint the enemies of my country.

I was not surprised that Wellington asked me to paint him. All powerful leaders love to control their image. Maybe I am wrong – maybe in your times this has stopped. Maybe your leaders no longer worry about their image and how they look to the wider world. Maybe … but I doubt it!

Thinking your enquiry through

Imagine you have been asked to paint a propaganda portrait of Napoleon. The request has come EITHER from Napoleon himself (in which case you must praise him) OR it could be from the British government (in which case your painting must disapprove of Napoleon).

Write a letter setting out what your portrait will show. You do not need to do a painting, but you could add some simple sketches. Just like David, you will need to decide what you will do about each of the following:

- **Context and action** - Where is Napoleon? What is he doing?

- **Pose** – What is Napoleon's stance? Where is he looking?

- **Expression** – How will his face tell us about his character?

- **Details** – How can possessions, clothing or scenery add extra information?

- **Lighting** – How can light and shade show eg power, hope or despair?

Above all you must show that you know about Napoleon's achievements and about his character. Who knows, you may even go on to paint a masterpiece!

'If only, if only...'

Why was Napoleon finally defeated at Waterloo?

For six years, between 1815 and 1821, a plump, brooding figure could be seen walking the windswept hillsides of the island of St Helena far out in the Atlantic ocean.

This was Napoleon Bonaparte. The French soldier-turned-Emperor, who had once controlled the whole of Europe from Spain to Russia, was ending his days as a prisoner on an island of no more than 47 square miles.

Napoleon on St Helena, an engraving, 1821

St Helena, an engraving, 1815

In all those lonely days on the island, Napoleon never came to terms with the defeat that had sent him to St Helena. In his mind he kept returning to 18 June 1815 when he and his French army were finally defeated at the Battle of Waterloo. After dinner one evening in 1816, a visitor asked him about the battle. Napoleon sighed with deep sorrow, shook his head and said "Incomprehensible day!"

Think

- The sketch above shows Napoleon on St Helena. Compare this with his portrait on page 117 (Crossing the Alps). Why do you think he looks so different?

- What do you think Napoleon meant when he called 18 June 1815 an "incomprehensible day"?

Winning an empire (1799 to 1807)

In 1799 Napoleon used his troops to take control of France. He believed that his country was in chaos and that he was the only man who could restore France to greatness.

As soon as he was in power, Napoleon set about destroying all France's enemies. He said he was trying protect France. He said he was spreading liberty to other people throughout Europe.

Not surprisingly, the four great monarchies of Europe despised Napoleon and went to war to end his rule. It took sixteen years of war before they succeeded.

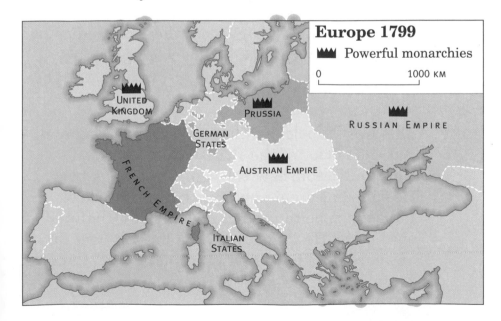

Europe 1799

👑 Powerful monarchies

0   1000 KM

UNITED KINGDOM

PRUSSIA

GERMAN STATES

RUSSIAN EMPIRE

AUSTRIAN EMPIRE

FRENCH EMPIRE

ITALIAN STATES

Think

- Use the map to name the four great monarchies of Europe

- What is a monarchy?

- Since 1793 France had been a republic. What is a republic?

- Why do you think France had so many enemies?

Napoleon met with rapid success in his wars on the continent. In 1800 his great victory at the Battle of Marengo gave him control of all Austria's lands in Italy. With Austria defeated, Russia and Prussia quickly gave up the struggle. Napoleon could now concentrate on the one remaining enemy, Great Britain … with her weak army and her all conquering navy.

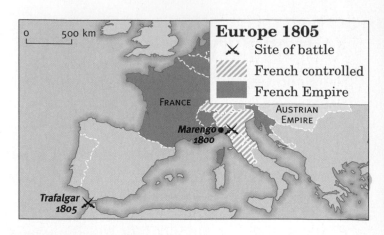

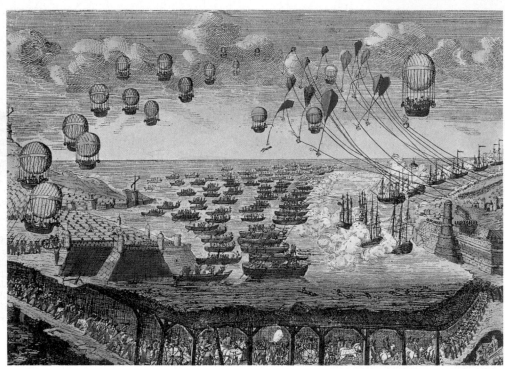

Napoleon was sure that he could beat the British army easily. But first he had to get his troops past the British navy and safely across the English Channel.

In 1803 he was making ambitious plans for an invasion of Britain. You can see some of his ideas in this French print from the time.

In 1805 Napoleon tried a simpler way of weakening the British navy's control over the Channel. He lured many of Britain's ships far away to the West Indies by pretending that French ships were going to attack Britain's wealthy sugar-producing islands there.

This was Napoleon's chance to invade England. But the leader of the British fleet, Admiral Horatio Nelson, saw through Napoleon's trick. He sailed at great speed back from the West Indies in time to protect the English Channel once more. He then forced the French fleet far away from Britain, finally trapping it at Cape Trafalgar off the coast of Spain.

Think

- Which part of the print shows France?

- Which part shows Britain?

- According to the picture, what were Napoleon's plans for invading Britain?

- Why do you think the print makes the English Channel look much narrower than it really is?

Napoleon had built a powerful army but had failed to improve the out-dated French navy. The French admiral complained that he had "bad masts, bad sails, bad officers and out-of-date tactics".

On 21 October 1805 at the Battle of Trafalgar, Nelson crushed the French fleet. The victory saved Britain – but it cost Nelson his life as a musket ball shattered his spine.

Nelson became a British national hero. This painting shows him being carried up to heaven.

Think

- Why was victory at Trafalgar so important to Britain?

- How has the artist, Legrand, made Nelson seem heroic?

- Which monument in London celebrates Nelson's victory?

The apotheosis of Nelson, a painting by Pierre Nicolas Legrand, early nineteenth century

The navy was one of Britain's two great strengths. The other was her enormous wealth. Her Prime Minister, William Pitt, used this wealth to pay Austria, Russia and Prussia to declare war again on France.

In 1805 these payments (known as "Pitt's cavalry") persuaded Austria and Russia to rejoin the war against France. Napoleon had to turn his armies away from the English Channel and march at great speed towards Austria.

The Plum Pudding in Danger, an English cartoon by James Gillray, 1805. Pitt is carving up the world's oceans while Napoleon takes the land.

Britain was undefeated but Napoleon quickly swept to victory against his other enemies. The chart below shows when, where and how he achieved his greatest successes.

Napoleon's victories	Europe 1807	Napoleon's tactics

Napoleon's victories

1. Austerlitz (December 1805). Napoleon beat a joint Austrian and Russian army.
2. Jena (October 1806). Napoleon beat the Prussians.
3. Friedland (June 1807). Napoleon beat the Russians.

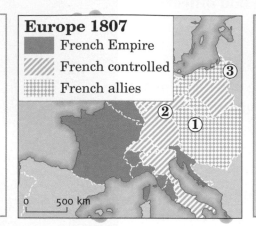

Europe 1807

- French Empire
- French controlled
- French allies

0   500 km

Napoleon's tactics

- He used large, well-trained armies.
- He moved his troops quickly, with crisp clear orders to each unit.
- He was quick and decisive at spotting weaknesses in his opponents' defences.

Victories such as these gave Napoleon his reputation as one of the greatest generals of all time. In these years he was at the peak of his powers … but he still had not defeated Britain.

STEP 1

Here is your first chance to make some "If only …" cards, like the ones shown here.

Despite his great success on mainland Europe, Napoleon later regretted his failure to defeat Britain by 1807. In the years ahead, Britain remained a constant problem.

Choose events from the section "Winning an empire" that you think **could** have helped Napoleon to defeat Britain **if only** they had turned out differently.

(A word of advice: good historians only consider realistic "If only" statements. Don't get carried away. Don't say "If only Napoleon had been able to use nuclear weapons").

If only Napoleon had improved the French navy as much as he improved the French army, perhaps he would have been able to invade Britain.

If only Napoleon had managed to build a tunnel under the English Channel, perhaps his army could have invaded Britain successfully.

Losing an empire (1807 to 1814)

By 1807 Napoleon more or less controlled every nation on the continent. He needed to keep them happy – **but he upset them one by one**.

Napoleon found it impossible to ignore his old rival across the English Channel. In 1807, Napoleon told all the countries of mainland Europe that they must not trade with Britain. He called this his "Continental System". The idea was that Britain's trade would be cut off and her wealth and power would be crippled for ever.

Of course, Britain retaliated. She used her navy to block the ports of any country that refused to trade with her. This meant that trade dried up in most of Europe. Prices rose ... and traders, customers and rulers all over Europe blamed Napoleon.

Think

- Why do you think Napoleon did not just ignore Britain?

- Do you think Britain would have attacked France if Napoleon left her alone?

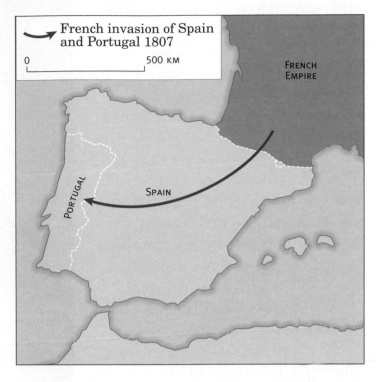

Napoleon's Continental System **annoyed the Portuguese**, who refused to join. Napoleon decided to teach them a lesson.

To attack the Portuguese Napoleon had to send an army through Spain. This army treated local people dreadfully, taking whatever supplies it needed without paying. When the Spanish complained, Napoleon forced them to accept his brother as their new king. This **insulted the Spanish**.

For the next six years, all over the peninsula of Spain and Portugal, ordinary men and women – as well as bandits and thieves – joined in a **guerrilla** war against the French.

These Spanish guerrillas avoided open battle. Instead they ambushed the French and then hid in villages and mountains. In retaliation, French soldiers sometimes lined up people they suspected of being rebels and shot them in cold blood.

The British sent an army to aid the Portuguese and Spanish in this 'Peninsula War'. The army was commanded by Sir Arthur Wellesley. Wellesley later became the Duke of Wellington – the man who finally beat Napoleon at Waterloo.

Between 1808 and 1814, Wellesley's army – and Spanish guerrilla tactics – forced Napoleon to keep over 250,000

French soldiers execute Spanish guerrillas, a painting by Goya 1814

soldiers in Spain. Napoleon was busy running his empire so he had to leave other generals in charge in Spain. But these generals lacked Napoleon's skill and could not end the war.

This long, costly struggle drained away so much money and so many soldiers that Napoleon called it his "Spanish ulcer", slowly eating away at his control over Europe.

To make matters worse, the French failure in Spain **provoked the Russians** to stand up against Napoleon. In 1810 the Russian Tsar (emperor) decided that his country's trade was being ruined by Napoleon's Continental System. He opened his ports to British ships. Napoleon could not allow this. He decided to invade Russia. Some say this was the greatest mistake he ever made.

Napoleon gathered over 650,000 men from all over his empire. It gave him the largest army the world had seen, but it **angered Germans, Dutch, Poles and many others** who had no real desire to fight for France.

Think

- What is guerrilla warfare?

- Why did the Peninsula War go on so long?

- Why was this war sometimes called the "Spanish ulcer?"

The Russians knew that Napoleon liked to fight pitched battles. So, instead of standing to fight, they retreated and destroyed their own people's crops and farms as they went. As the French army pushed deeper into Russia, thousands of its soldiers starved, died of disease or deserted.

When Napoleon finally reached Moscow, he found the city in flames. The Russians had burned their own capital to the ground rather than see it fall into French hands.

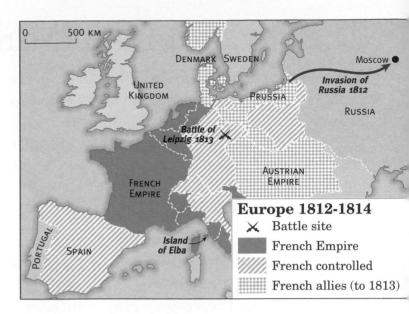

Europe 1812-1814
✗ Battle site
French Empire
French controlled
French allies (to 1813)

Think

- Some people say that Napoleon's army was too big for its own good. How could this be true?

- Some historians say the Russian winter defeated Napoleon in 1812. Do you agree?

Napoleon could not stay in Moscow without supplies or shelter. He ordered a retreat. A bitterly cold winter closed in on his army and only 20,000 men returned to France alive. Napoleon had never been weaker.

In 1813, a joint force of Austrians, Russians, Prussians and Swedes defeated Napoleon at the Battle of Leipzig. Meanwhile the British invaded France from Spain. Napoleon's empire was collapsing.

In 1814 Napoleon surrendered and on 27 April he was sent away to live on the island of Elba, off the west coast of Italy.

But if anyone thought they had defeated Napoleon for ever, they were very wrong.

STEP 2

If only the war in Spain had ended more quickly, no one else would have dared to challenge Napoleon.

Napoleon must have wondered whether he could have kept his great European empire, **if only** some things had happened differently.

Use the section "Losing an empire" to make some more **if only** cards like the one shown here.

The Hundred Days (March to June 1815)

It **seemed** that Napoleon had been defeated so the dead king's brother, Louis XVIII returned to rule France. But, in spring 1815, Napoleon escaped from Elba. He landed in the south of France with a few hundred loyal troops. Over the next two weeks he marched north to the sound of cheering crowds. King Louis fled and on 20 March Napoleon entered Paris.

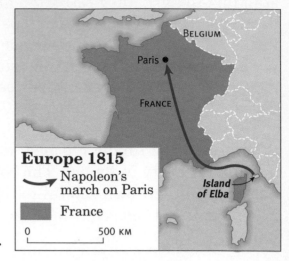

Europe 1815

⌒ Napoleon's march on Paris

▮ France

0 ———— 500 KM

Napoleon promised that he simply wanted to rule France in peace. The rulers of Britain, Austria, Russia and Prussia did not believe a word of it. They agreed to join forces and to destroy Napoleon once and for all.

The British sent the Duke of Wellington to Belgium to lead an army made up of soldiers from Britain and several smaller European states. The Prussians, Austrians and Russians also prepared to attack France.

Napoleon could see that he was going to have to fight one more war. He quickly gathered an army and set off to confront Wellington's force.

Facts about Napoleon's army	Facts about Wellington's army

Facts about Napoleon's army

- Napoleon had 120,000 quite experienced, loyal French volunteers
- The army was less well equipped than Napoleon's earlier forces
- Some of Napoleon's best generals from earlier wars were either dead or too old to use.
- Napoleon's two most experienced generals (Soult and Ney) loathed each other

Facts about Wellington's army

- Wellington led 58,000 soldiers – mainly inexperienced British men, supported by others from eg Holland and Belgium
- Many of Wellington's best soldiers had been sent to Canada in 1814
- Wellington mixed his best British soldiers with less experienced men
- Wellington hoped to join forces with the Prussian army of 84,000 men in Belgium.

Think

- What do you think were the strengths of each army?
- What do you think were the weaknesses of each army?
- Which army do you think should have been most confident of winning?

Napoleon knew that he must not allow his enemies to combine their armies. He wanted to pick them off one by one, starting with the British and Prussians who planned to meet in Belgium. This map shows how he set about this task

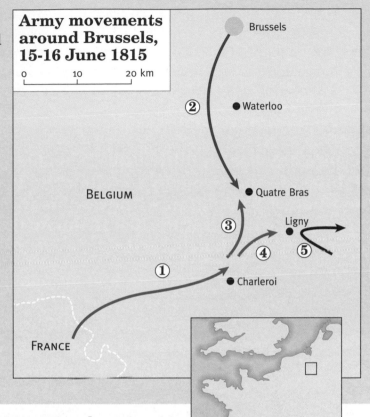

1 - At dawn on 15 June, Napoleon marched his army at great speed into Belgium and occupied a position between the British and Prussians. Wellington learned about Napoleon's surprise move that evening, but calmly attended a grand ball in Brussels before re-joining his own army later that night.

2 - On 16 June Wellington moved his men south from Brussels, trying to join up with the Prussian army under Prince Blucher.

3 - Napoleon sent Marshall Ney with 24,000 troops to block the British at the village of Quatre Bras.

4 - Napoleon himself took the main French army and defeated the Prussians at Ligny.

5 - The Prussians fled from the battlefield ... but Napoleon chose not to follow them.

Earlier in his career, the young, quick-thinking Napoleon would probably have followed the retreating Prussians to crush them mercilessly. On this occasion he did not. Instead, he waited until the next day (17 June) and sent his least experienced general, Grouchy, with 33,000 men to find and follow the retreating Prussians. He gave Grouchy these orders:

You will pursue the enemy. Observe his march and tell me of his movements. It is important to discover what Wellington and Blucher mean to do, whether they want to unite their armies.

Think

- Which of the following do you think Grouchy was supposed to do when he found the Prussians?

  a) Fight them

  b) Send a report to Napoleon

  c) Return with all his men to Napoleon

- Does it surprise you that Napoleon sent 33,000 men with Grouchy? Explain your answer.

By 1815 Napoleon had grown fat. As his body slowed up so did his mind. He also had many health problems.

- His left leg felt the pain of an old bayonet wound.
- A bladder infection regularly caused him agony while urinating.
- He had an unpleasant skin infection which caused terrible itching and led him to sit for hours in baths of warm water.
- On the night of 16-17 June he had a painful attack of piles. His surgeon probably treated him by applying flannels soaked in warm water or by using leeches to suck the blood from the swollen veins around his anus.

Despite any health difficulties, Napoleon was up early on 17 June to send Grouchy to follow the Prussians. Meanwhile, the Duke of Wellington withdrew his troops to a site near a little village called Waterloo. He knew that the landscape there suited his battle tactics.

If Napoleon had attacked Wellington's army as it was moving position, the French would surely have won. But Wellington spread a screen of cavalry across the rest of his army and disguised his movements.

By nightfall on 17 June, Napoleon and Wellington both knew that the next day they would face each other in battle for the very first time. The outcome would decide the future of Europe.

STEP 3

If only Napoleon had been able to use more experienced generals he would have had a better chance of winning.

Years later, on the island of St Helena, Napoleon must have looked back on the days leading up to the Battle of Waterloo. He must have wondered how his chances of winning would have been improved if only some things had been different.

Use the section "The Hundred Days" to make some more if only cards like the one shown here.

The Incomprehensible Day (18 June 1815)

Early on the morning of 18 June, Napoleon met his generals for breakfast. They were worried. Some had fought against Wellington in Spain and had lost. Napoleon snapped at them saying …

> "Because you have been beaten by Wellington, you consider him a great general. I tell you that Wellington is a bad general, that the English are bad troops and that this battle will be over in a morning"

Think

● Does this statement by Napoleon prove that he was overconfident going into battle at Waterloo?

The battle was not over by lunch time. In fact the fighting had barely started by midday. A thunderstorm overnight made Napoleon delay his attack on Wellington for about three hours. He had to let the ground dry out so that he could move his cannon into position.

Early that day, Wellington received a message from Prince Blucher. The Prussian army was on its way to join him. It would have to struggle through eight miles of mud-filled farm lanes but if Wellington could hold off Napoleon's attacks until Blucher arrived, he would gain 30,000 men and surely win the day.

Wellington spread his troops across a hillside in a strong, defensive formation, hiding many of them from the French in a slight hollow. He mixed reliable troops with less experienced men. He occupied farm buildings to hold back any French attacks as long as possible.

Think

● Do you think the thunderstorm helped Wellington?

● Why do you think Wellington hid thousands of troops in the hollow?

● Do you think Wellington was wise to take up such a defensive position?

At about 11.30am Napoleon ordered his men to attack. **The Battle of Waterloo had started**. Many miles away, General Grouchy heard the gunfire. He wondered whether he should re-join Napoleon but decided to carry on following the Prussian army … and eating strawberries.

The Battle of Waterloo saw nine hours of mud, blood, noise and death. Throughout this time **Wellington** rode around energetically, encouraging his troops and giving orders in person. On several occasions people within a few feet of him were killed. One of his deputies had his leg blown off while in the middle of a conversation with Wellington. After the battle, Wellington wrote "the finger of Providence was upon me".

Napoleon behaved very differently. He remained behind his army and was far less active, sending frustrated orders to Ney and Soult his two deputies. Sometimes he wanted them to attack when they wanted to defend. Sometimes he complained that they were being too aggressive. At other times he wondered why they did not show more initiative. Above all he wondered why Grouchy had not returned to help him.

Think

- Why do you think Grouchy did not re-join Napoleon?

- What did Wellington mean by "the finger of Providence?"

The Battle of Waterloo, a painting by Dighton, (1792-1827)

For over five hours, Wellington's army kept up its grim defence against French attacks. At one point, about 16,000 French infantry almost made a breakthrough. They marched up the hill into the centre of the British lines only to be cut down by rifle fire from Wellington's second force hidden behind the slope. A British cavalry charge finished them off.

At about 5.00pm Prince Blucher's Prussian troops finally reached the battlefield. Wellington gained 30,000 men, just when he was desperate for reinforcements. Grouchy and the 30,000 French troops who had been sent by Napoleon to follow these Prussians were nowhere to be seen.

From the time Blucher arrived, Wellington had the advantage. It still took several more hours of attack and counter-attack before he was sure that the French army was too weak to continue. At 8.00pm Wellington gave the orders for the British infantry to advance. He told them, "No cheering my lads but forward and complete your victory". They pressed home their advantage and the French retreated in disarray. **Napoleon had lost**.

All over the smoke-filled battlefield of Waterloo lay 50,000 dead. Fields, ditches and lanes were filled with corpses. In place of the gunfire, drumming, bugling and screams of battle, there arose a long continuous moan from the wounded.

Battle of Waterloo ... some grim facts

- c. 15,000 of Wellington's men died
- c. 7,000 Pussians died
- c. 28,000 Frenchmen died
- c. 10,000 horses died
- Many wounded soldiers lay buried by dead bodies for three days before they were pulled out alive.
- Parties of scavengers roamed the field, robbing the corpses and even murdering the wounded of both sides to take their valuables
- Tourists were visiting the battlefield within three weeks
- A souvenir trade quickly grew up selling musket balls taken from walls and trees. Later, the hooves of Napoleon's horse were turned into snuffboxes.

Napoleon escaped and made his way back to Paris. He wanted to sail to America, but British ships controlled the French ports. Within a month he gave himself up to the British.

In October 1815, a British ship landed him on the island of St Helena. From then until his death in 1821, his mind kept returning to the "incomprehensible day" when he lost the Battle of Waterloo and how things might have been so very different "if only, if only …"

Napoleon must have wondered whether he could have won the battle of Waterloo **if only** some things had been different on that day.

Use the section "The Incomprehensible Day" to make some more **if only** cards like the one shown here.

If only rain had not yet delayed the start of the battle, Napoleon might have won before the Prussians arrived.

Thinking your enquiry through

By now you should have a good collection of "If only" cards. You will need to use these to help you prepare for your dinner party with Napoleon. Napoleon (who may bear a strange resemblance to your history teacher) will be asking you to show how history could have been very different if only certain events had turned out differently.

1 To help you get ready for your meal with Napoleon, decide which cards can help you answer each of these questions:

   a) "Could I have kept power **if only** luck had been on my side?"

   b) "Could I have kept power **if only** my opponents had acted differently?"

   c) "Could I have kept power **if only** I had made better decisions?"

2 Napoleon will also ask you to answer two more very tricky questions. Have some good answers ready!

   a) "Why do you think I lost power?"

   b) "Is there any point in looking back on history and saying "If only"?"

'So what?'

What has studying the French Revolution done for you?

History is the 'people' subject. By studying what people have done in the past we can make more sense of the way the world works and of the people who live in it.

Here is a very simple summary of the story of the French Revolution. The red words scattered around it capture some important ideas and human qualities. Now tackle the tasks on page 143.

Human nature

The story of the …
In the years leading up to the French Revolution, King Louis XVI and rich nobles ruled the nation. Ordinary people (called the Third Estate) paid all the taxes but had no say in how France was governed.

The story of the Tennis Court Oath
In 1789 the King needed even more money. The Third Estate said they would only pay new taxes if the King cut his own power. The King was desperate for money so, in June 1789, he agreed to rule through a National Assembly (an elected parliament).

The story of the Bastille
On 14 July 1789 thousands of people in Paris "stormed" one of the King's fortresses looking for weapons. They feared that the King was going to use his army to end the National Assembly. Since then books, films and annual holidays celebrate the "Storming of the Bastille" as the start of the French Revolution.

The story of the King's death
In October 1789 the National Assembly agreed a Declaration of the Rights of Man and the Citizen. This set out how all people were to be treated equally and fairly. King Louis was losing control. By 1792 no one seemed to be in control as crowds in Paris massacred thousands of nobles, priests and royal supporters. After a one-sided trial, Louis was executed by guillotine in January 1793.

Fear

Sacrifice

Fairness

Greed

Courage

Law

142

Responsibilities

Pride

The story of the Terror

In 1793-94 up to 25,000 people were put to death in France for not supporting the Revolution. Robespierre claimed that he had to destroy all opposition or the people of France would lose their newly won freedom and equality. New laws and new courts made it easy to arrest and execute anyone who upset the government. Churches were closed. In 1794 Robespierre was executed by his rivals.

The story of women

The Revolution did not give women the right to vote or to take part in the National Assembly. They did gain new rights in divorce cases and were given equal rights to inherit property. Many women also joined in demonstrations, protests and riots. Most women simply carried on trying to feed and care for their families.

Selfishness

The story of Napoleon's leadership of France

In 1799 a soldier called Napoleon used force to take control of the government. For the next sixteen years he ruled the country more or less as a dictator. He told artists to paint him as a powerful genius so that people would support him. He made many reforms that helped France, but he reduced women's rights and banned anyone from criticising him in newspapers.

The story of Napoleon's wars

Napoleon conquered nearly the whole of Europe. He wanted to crush any nation that dared to oppose France. He claimed that he was spreading French ideas about freedom in the countries he conquered. He said he wanted to create a single, united Europe. In the end he made so many enemies that they joined against him and defeated him at Waterloo in 1815. The age of the French Revolution was over.

Service

Justice

Conflict

Ambition

Work in pairs. Each pair must take a different red word.

1 **Identify events from the French Revolution that are connected with your word. You should find plenty!**

2 **Join another pair. Discuss how your two words are connected.**

3 **Discuss how studying the French Revolution has deepened your understanding of any of these words.**

Glossary

Absolute authority — Authority not shared with anyone else

Ancien Regime — Old system of government before the French Revolution

Assembly of Notables — A gathering of important noblemen

Cabinet — A meeting (in Britain) of the King or Queen's most important advisers

Cahiers de doléances — Notebooks of complaints that the people of France were asked to write before the Estates General met

Censored — Edited e.g. by government agents who try to control what people read

Concordat — An agreement between Napoleon and the Pope

Constitution — A document which states the rules within which a government must govern

Controller general — The minister in charge of the King's finances in France

Counter-revolution — An attempt to turn back all the changes made by a revolution

Coup d'etat — A sudden change of government carried out by force

Courtiers — Noble men and women who attend court

Dauphin — The heir to the throne

Decree — A government order

Deficit — The money that a person or a government owes when they have spent more than they earn

Deputies — People chosen as representatives

Dictatorship — A system of government where one person (a dictator) has complete control

Election — Choosing representatives or leaders by voting

Enlightenment — A new way of thinking that developed in the eighteenth century

Estates — All people in France belonged to one of the three estates

Estates General — A special meeting of elected representatives of each of the three estates

Exiled — Required to leave the country by law as a punishment

Feudal — The feudal system was an old arrangement where people received land in return for doing some sort of work for their lord or King

Finances — Money matters

Guerrilla — A soldier who fights by ambushes and quick raids not by pitched battles

Lettre de cachet	A secret letter used by the King and his advisers to imprison people without a trial	**Patriotic**	Standing up proudly for your country
Messiah	A saviour sent by God	*Philosophes*	Educated men in the eighteenth century who wrote about ways of creating a better, fairer society
Metaphor	Describing something as though it is something else (for example, referring to France as though it were a building under attack: "Her strongest towers collapsed"	**Plebiscite**	A national vote to decide one particular issue
		Propaganda	Spreading one-sided messages to control public opinion
Myth	A story that is fictional or has not been proven to be true. It might be a story that carries an important meaning for a group of people, even if the factual details are incorrect	**Representatives**	Someone who is acting on behalf of other people
		Republic	A country which has no monarch
		Revenge	Getting your own back in an angry or nasty way
National Assembly	The assembly of deputies which ruled France from June 1789	*Sans culottes*	Men who did not wear the knee breeches worn by the bourgeoisie. Ordinary people active in the revolution were called sans culottes ('without breeches') after 1791
National Guard	A kind of citizens' police force		
Parlement	Special French law-courts where new laws were registered		
Parliament	A regular meeting (in Britain) of the representatives from all over the country and of the King or Queen's advisers to make laws or discuss problems in the country. France did not have a parliament	**Tithes**	Taxes paid to the church
		Tyranny	Cruel government, usually by one person
		Veto	The right to reject a new law

Index

absolute authority 18–19

ancien regime 19, 24

Assembly of Notables 28–9, 33

Bastille 42–65, 142

Bastille Day 63–4

Battle of Leipzig 133

Battle of Marengo 116, 128

Battle of Trafalgar 128–29

Battle of Waterloo 125, 134–41

Blucher, Prince 135–41

Bonaparte, Napoleon 112–43, 143
  Emperor 120–1
  French Empire 122–41
  Hundred Days 134–6
  reforms 118–19
  rise to power 115–17

bourgeoisie 8

bread 14–16

Britain 86, 128

cahiers de doléances 6, 15, 22, 36

Calonne 28–9

Carlyle, Thomas 53

censorship 118

church 73, 90, 94, 106, 118, 123

citizens 20, 61, 96–111

clergy 10, 11

Code Napoleon 118, 123

Committee of Public Safety 87–95

complaints system 6–9, 18–22

conscription 86, 89

Constitution 40, 76

Continental System 131–2

Controller-General 19

Convention, The 78, 80, 83, 87, 110

Corday, Charlotte 113

corvée 12–13

coups d'etat 116

Danton, George 94

David, Jacques Louis 112–25

Day of Tiles 34

De Launay 49, 58, 67

Declaration of the Rights of Man and the Citizen 68, 71, 103–5

Declaration of the Rights of Women 105

depositions 100–1

deputies, Estates General 6

Desmoulins, Camille 56

Dickens, Charles 42–52, 55–6, 60

dowries 96–7, 99

Drouet 74–5

drought 15, 33, 69

drownings 92–3

Ducroquet, Harlay 108

economic changes 106

economic terror 89

education 97, 99, 118

elections 6

Enlightenment 20–2

equality 103–4

Estate system 10–13

Estates General 18, 29, 34
  deputies 6
  Réveillon riots 16
  Tennis Court Oath 27

voting system 23–5, 35

women 98

feudal rights 13, 68, 71, 123

finances, King Louis XVI 28–9

First Estate 10

Fouche, Joseph 92

French Empire 122–39

Girondists 76, 87

Glain, Madeline 101

Gouge, Marie (Olympe de Gouges) 105, 107

government 18–22, 106

Great Terror 94–5

Gros, Antoine-Jean 119

Grouchy 137–43

guerrilla wars 131–2

guillotine 82, 87, 92, 94–5

Guinee, Anne 109

hailstorm 33

harvests, weather 15

Hebert, Jaques 94

hoarding grain 89, 94, 100

Hundred Days 134–6

inflation 86

Jacobins 76–8, 87

King Louis XVI 66–81, 142
  deposed 76–8
  escape attempt 74–5
  execution 81
  finances 28–9
  imprisonment 78
  National Assembly 67–8, 71
  powers 18–23
  trial 79–80
  troops in Paris 39, 55–7

Tuileries 72–3, 74, 77, 78

King Louis XVIII 136

landlords 12–13

landowners 17, 29

Law of General Maximum 89

Law of Suspects 91

laws, complaints system 18–22

Legion of Honour 118

lettres de cachet 18

Levee en Masse 89

liberty 63, 65, 103–4

Lycees 118

Marat, Jean-Paul 113

march to Versailles 70–1, 100

Marie Antoinette, Queen 20, 70–2, 74–5, 79–80, 91

marriage contracts 96–7, 99

mass drownings 92–3

massacre at the Tuileries 78

Michelet 52

Mirabeau 40

Napoleon see Bonaparte, Napoleon

National Assembly 35
  Declaration of the Rights of Man and the Citizen 68, 71
  defies the King 38–41
  feudal rights 68, 71

Necker 16, 29, 33, 57

Nelson, Admiral Horatio 130–1

nobility 8, 10, 11, 22

nobility of the robe 10

nobility of the sword 10

October Days 100
Paris Parlement 32–4
Parlements 18, 29, 32–4
peasants 9, 12–13
Peninsula War 131–2
petitions to the King 99, 109
philosophes 20–2, 54
Place de la Revolution 80
plebiscites 116, 119, 120
political terror 91–3
Portugal 131–2
price controls 87
privileges 8–9
propaganda 114
Prussia 77, 86, 130–1, 134–139
rebellion 86
religious terror 90
Republican Petition 76
Réveillon riots 16–17
revenge 44–5, 65
Revolt of the Nobles 33
Revolutionary Tribunal 91–5
rights 8–9
  feudal 13, 68, 71, 123
  women 103–5
riots 16–17, 33, 34, 100
Robespierre, Maximilien 82–95, 143
  character 84–5
  Committee of Public Safety 87–95
  economic terror 89
  execution 94
  Great Terror 94–5
  political terror 91–3
  religious terror 90

Rousseau, Jean-Jacques 20, 22
Royal Session 38
Russia 129, 132–134
salt tax 6–7
Sans Culottes 61–2, 77, 78, 86–7, 90–1, 110
sealed letters 18
Second Estate 10
September Massacres 78
Sieyès, Abbé 23, 24, 36
social changes 106
social contracts 20
Spain 86, 131–2
taille 7, 12
Tale of Two Cities, A 42–52, 55–6, 60
taxation 6–7, 12–13
Tennis Court Oath 26–31, 38, 142
Terror 82–95, 143
  Committee of Public Safety 87–95
  economic terror 89
  Great Terror 94–5
  political terror 91–3
  religious terror 90
  women 108–10
Third Estate 10, 16, 23–5, 35–7
Three Estates 10–13
tithes 7
town workers 9, 60
Tricolore 61, 69
Tuileries 72–3, 74, 77, 78
Turgot 29
unemployment 14, 15, 69
Universal Declaration of Human Rights 104
Vendée 86, 92–3
Versailles 19, 26–7,

70–1, 100
Voltaire, Francois-Marie 21, 22
Wellington, Duke of 125, 132, 134–43
women 96–111, 145
  Bonaparte, Napoleon 118
  Declaration of the Rights of Man and the Citizen 103–5
  depositions 100–1
  events of 1789 98–102
  march to Versailles 70–1, 100
  petitions to the King 99, 109
  political clubs 104
  Terror 108–10

Acknowledgements

The Art Archive/Musée des Arts Decoratifs, Paris/Dagli Orti: p.8b, The Art Archive/Musée Carnavalet, Paris/Marc Charmet: p.81, The Art Archive/Musée Carnavalet, Paris/Dagli Orti: pp.26,103,113, The Art Archive: p.116, The Art Archive/Musée du Chateau de Versailles/Dagli Orti: p.66, The Art Archive/Marc Charmet: pp.72,91, The Art Archive/Musée du Louvre, Paris/Dagli Orti: p.96; Bibliothéque Nationale, Paris: p.114b; 'The Blood of the Murdered Crying for Vengeance', the execution of Louis XVI by guillotine, by James Gillray, courtesy of the Warden and Scholars of New College, Oxford/Bridgeman Art Library: p.5, The Penthievre Family or The Cup of Chocolate, Chateau de Versailles, France/BAL: p.8t, Archives Charmet/BAL: 9t, Musée de la ville de Paris, Musée Carnavalet, Paris/BAL: pp.11, 18, 58, 83, Lauros/Giraudon/BAL: pp.12, 16, 19, 61, 84, Marie Antoinette with a Rose, by Louise Elizabeth Vigee-Lebrun, 1783, Lauros/Giraudon/BAL: pp.20t, Giraudon/BAL: pp.20b, 21, 94r,112, Charles Alexandre de Calonne, by Johann Ernst Heinsius, Giraudon/BAL: p.28, Visual Arts Library/Musée de la Revolution/BAL: p.34, Archives Charmet/BAL: p.37, 'A Versailles, A Versailles', March of the Women on Versailles, Paris, Lauros/Giraudon/BAL: p.70, Plunder of a Church During the Revolution, Visual Arts Library, London/BAL: p.90, Siege of Lyon, October 1793, Lauros/Giraudon/BAL: p.92, Episode in Place du Bouffay, Nantes, 1793, by Auguste Hyacinthe Debay, 1859, Giraudon/BAL: p.93, Robespierre Guillotining the Executioner, c.1793, by French School 18th century, Private Collection/BAL: p.95, Opening of the Estates General at Versailles, 5th May 1789, by Louis Charles Auguste Couder, Giraudon/BAL: p.98, The Triumphant Parisian Army Returning to Paris from Versailles, 6th October 1789, Lauros/Giraudon/BAL: p.100, Women's Patriotic Club, by Le Sueur Brothers, 18th century, Musée de la ville de Paris, Musée Carnavalet, Paris/BAL: pp.104, 106, Madame Aubry, Olympia of Gouges, 1784, French School 18th century, Musée de la ville de Paris, Musée Carnavalet, Paris/BAL: p.105, View of the Elevated Mountain at the Champ de la Reunion for the Festival of the Supreme Being, 1794, by French School 18th century, Visual Arts Library, London/BAL: p.114t, Unfinished portrait of General Bonaparte, c.1797-98, by Jacques Louis David, Giraudon/BAL: p.115, Napoleon Crossing the Alps at the St Bernard Pass, 20th May 1800, by Jacques Louis David, Lauros/Giraudon/BAL: p.117, Napoleon Bonaparte visiting the Plague Stricken of Jaffa, 11th March 1799, by Baron Antoine Jean Gros, 1804, Louvre, Paris/BAL: p.119, The Consecration of the Emperor Napoleon and the Coronation of the Empress Josephine, by Pope Pius VII, 1804, Louvre, Paris/BAL: p.121, The Distribution of the Eagle Standards, 5th December 1804, detail of the Standard Bearers, by Jacques Louis David, 1808-10, Giraudon/BAL: p.122, Napoleon Bonaparte in his Study, 1812, by Jacques Louis David, Kress Collection, Washington D.C/BAL: p.124, Ideas for an Attack on England, by French School 19th century, Collection Kharbine-Tapabor, Paris/BAL: p.128, Ferens Art Gallery, Hull City Museums and Art Galleries/BAL: p.129t, Private Collection/BAL: pp.129b, 138-139, Execution of the Defenders of Madrid, 3rd May 1808, by Francisco Jose de Goya y Lucientes, 1814, Prado, Madrid/BAL: p.132; Source: The British Film Institute: pp.47,50; MEPL/Explorer: p.80, MEPL: p.94l; Hulton | Archive: pp.9b, 44;
Peter Newark's Historical Pictures: pp.21b, 126l; Photos12.com-ARJ: p.79; Sipa Press/Rex Features: p.63; Sotheby's Picture Library, London: p.133; Tate, London 2003: p.131; Roger Viollet: p.126r.

We have been unable to trace the copyright of the images on pages 47, 50, and would be grateful for any information that would enable us to do so.

Cover: Bettmann/CORBIS

Original written sources have been simplified where necessary.

Pearson Education Limited
Edinburgh Gate
Harlow
Essex CM20 2JE
England

First published 2003

ISBN 0582 535905

Designed by Jennifer Coles
Illustrated by Kathy Baxendale, Mark Oldroyd, Chris Rothero and David Shenton.
Picture Research by Sandie Huskinson-Rolfe of Photoseekers

Printed in UK by Scotprint Ltd, Haddington.

The Publishers' policy is to use paper manufactured from sustainable forests.